Helion & Company Limited
Unit 8 Amherst Business Centre
Budbrooke Road
Warwick
CV34 5WE
England
Tel. 01926 499 619
Email: info@helion.co.uk
Website: www.helion.co.uk
Twitter: @helionbooks
Visit our blog http://blog.helion.co.uk/

Designed & typeset by Farr out Publications, Wokingham, Berkshire
Cover design Paul Hewitt, Battlefield Design (www.battlefield-design.co.uk)
Printed by Henry Ling Limited, Dorchester, Dorset

ISBN 978-1-912866-35-9

British Library Cataloguing-in-Publication Data
A catalogue record for this book is available from the British Library

CONTENTS

Abbreviations 2
Preface 3

1 Background and Context 4
2 RV i PVO on the Eve of the War 13
3 War in Slovenia 31
4 Crisis in Croatia 51
5 Counter-Air Operations 65
6 All-Out War 69

Bibliography 85
Notes 86
About the Author 88

Note: in order to simplify the use of this book, all names, locations and geographic designations are as provided in *The Times World Atlas*, or other traditionally accepted major sources of reference, as of the time of the described events. All military ranks are as in official use at the time of the described events. Unless stated otherwise, all times are local times. While only the first letter of official designations of institutions and services of the Yugoslav armed forces was written in capital letters, and this practice was subsequently adopted in Croatia and Slovenia, their translations in this book are written as usual in the English language. When mentioned for the first time in the text, aircraft and heavy weapons system designations are cited fully – including their designer and/or the manufacturer, official military designation and nickname: in the case of Soviet-made armament: this is followed by the ASCC/NATO-codename, but through the text only their original designations are used. Local, Yugoslav designations are provided in separate tables. Unless cited in the endnotes, all sources are interviews with participants or original documentation listed in the bibliography.

For easier understanding of ranks of the Yugoslav air force used in this book, herewith a table comparing these with ranks in the US Air Force and the Royal Air Force (United Kingdom) from the highest-non-commissioned-officer-rank, to the highest officer rank.

RV i PVO	US Air Force	Royal Air Force (United Kingdom)
	General of the Army (5-star)	Marshal of the Royal Air Force
general armije/General of the Army (4-star)	General (4-star)	Air Chief Marshal
general-pukovnik/Colonel-General (3-star)	Lieutenant-General (3-star)	Air Marshal
general-potpukovnik/Lieutenant-General (2-star)	Major-General (2-star)	Air Vice Marshal
general-major/Major-General (1-star)	Brigadier-General (1-star)	Air Commodore
pukovnik/Colonel	Colonel	Group Captain
potpukovnik/Lieutenant-Colonel	Lieutenant-Colonel	Wing Commander
major/Major	Major	Squadron Leader
kapetan 1. klase/Captain 1st Class		
kapetan/Captain	Captain	Flight Lieutenant
poručnik/1st Lieutenant	1st Lieutenant	Flying Officer
potporučnik/2nd Lieutenant	2nd Lieutenant	Pilot Officer
zastavnik 1. klase/Warrant Officer 1st Class	Chief Master Sergeant of the Air Force	Master Aircrew

ABBREVIATIONS

AB air base
An Antonov (the design bureau led by Oleg Antonov)
AoR area of responsibility
AMD-BA Avions Marcel Dassault – Breguet Aviation
APC armoured personnel carrier
ATAF Allied Tactical Air Force (NATO)
ATC air traffic control (in the SFRJ, this was a combined, civilian-military authority, directed by a military officer with a rank of general)
BAe British Aerospace (nowadays BAE Systems)
BAI battlefield air interdiction
C-SAR combat search and rescue
CAP combat air patrol
CAS close air support
CIA Central Intelligence Agency (USA)
COMINT communications intelligence
ECM electronic countermeasures
ECCM electronic counter-countermeasures
ECMM European Community Monitor Mission
ELINT electronic intelligence
FLIR Forward Looking Infrared
GCI ground-controlled intercept/ion
HAS hardened aircraft shelter
HDD head-down display
HDZ Hrvatska demokratska zajednica (Croat political party)
HE high explosive
HEAT high-explosive anti-tank
HOS Hrvatske odbrambene snage (Croat Defence Forces, armed wing of the HSP)
HQ Headquarters
HRM Hrvatska ratna mornarica (Croat Navy)
HRZ i PZO Hrvatsko ratno zrakoplovstvo (Croat Air Force and Air Defence, official designation since 12 December 1991)
HUD head-up display
HV Hrvatska vojska (Croat Army, since 1995)
IFV infantry fighting vehicle
IAP international airport
ICTY International Criminal Tribunal for the former Yugoslavia
IrAF Iraqi Air Force
JNA Jugoslovenska narodna armija (Yugoslav armed forces – all branches/in general – and colloquial for the Yugoslav army/ground forces, 1952-1991)
JRM colloquial for RM
JRV i PVO colloquial for RV i PVO
kN Kilo-Newton
Kosmet colloquial for 'Kosovo i Metohija' (former autonomous province in southern Serbia)
KoV Kopnena vojska (JNA's ground forces)
LORAP Long Range Aerial Photography
LOROP Long Range Oblique Photography
MANPADS man-portable air defence system
MBT main battle tank
MD Military District ('Vojna oblast' in the JNA)
MDAP Mutual Defense Aid Program
MiG Mikoyan i Gurevich (the design bureau led by Artyom Ivanovich Mikoyan and Mikhail Iosifovich Gurevich, also known as OKB-155 or MMZ 'Zenit')
MSNZ Manevarske strukture narodne zaščite (Manoeuvre Structures of National Defence, Slovenia)
MUP Ministry of Interior (ministry of inner affairs)
NATO North Atlantic Treaty Organisation
NCO/s non-commissioned officer/s
OG Operativna Grupa (Task Force)

QRA	Quick Reaction Alert
PA	Privredna avijacija (agrar aviation)
POW	prisoner of war
PVO	Protivovozdushnaya Oborona Strany (Soviet Air Defence Force)
RAF	Royal Air Force (of the United Kingdom)
RM	Ratna mornarica (official designation for the navy, 1952-1991)
RPG	rocket-propelled grenade
RV i PVO	Ratno vazduhoplovstvo i protivvazdušna odbrana (official designation, 1959-1991)
SAM	surface-to-air missile
SAO	Samostalna autonomna oblast (Independent Autonomous Region; political organisation of the Serb-controlled parts of Croatia, 1990-1991)
SDB	Služba državne bezbednosti (State Security Service)
SEM	Specialna enota milice (Special Police Unit, Slovenia)
SFRJ	Socijalistička Federativna Republika Jugoslavija (Socialist Federative Republic of Yugoslavia)
SHS	(Kraljevina) Srba, Hrvata i Slovenaca (Kingdom of Serbs, Croats and Slovenes; official designation of the future Yugoslavia, 1918-1929)
SIGINT	signals intelligence
SIV	Savezno izvršno veće (Federal Executive Council, 8-member presidency of the SFRJ)
SSNO	Savezni sekretarijat za narodnu odbranu (Federal Secretariat for National Defence; SFRJ's equivalent to the Ministry of Defence, 1971-1992)
SSUP	Savezni sekretarijat unutrašnjih poslova (Federal Secretariat for Internal Affairs; SFRJ's equivalent to the Ministry of Interior, 1971-1992
ŠVK	Štab vrhovne komande (High command, JNA, established in January 1991)
SZUP	Služba za zaštitu ustavnog poretka (Service for Protection of Constitutional Order; Croat Secret Service)
TO	Teritorijalna odbrana (Territorial Defence)
TOS	Teritorialna obramba Slovenije (TO of Slovenia)
UN	United Nations
USA	United States of America
USAF	United States Air Force
USN	United States Navy
USSR	Union of Soviet Socialist Republics (also 'Soviet Union')
VSJ	Varzduhoplovni savez Jugoslavije (Aeronautic Association of Yugoslavia)
VTI	Vazduhoplovnotehnički institut (Aeronautic Technical Institute)
VVA	Vazduhoplovna vojna akademija (Air Force Academy of the RV i PVO)
VVS	Voyenno-Vozdushnye Sily (Soviet Air Force)
ZNG	Zbor narodne garde (Croat National Guard, 1991-1994)
Yak	Yakovlev (the design bureau led by Alexander Sergeyevich Yakovlev)

PREFACE

The authors of books on contemporary military history usually work themselves through thousands of pages of documents and interviews with participants and eyewitnesses. As they go, they are recording not only facts – but emotions, too. Certainly enough, there are exceptions: sometimes, authors manage to establish an emotional distance. I can't: at the time of the war described in this volume, I was living in Zadar, a town on the coast of the Adriatic Sea, near Zemunik Air Base (AB), and I hung out with officers and other ranks, with students of the Air Force Academy (Vazduhoplovna vojna akademija, VVA) – all of whom were enthusiasts of flying and aircraft. The first year of the war had already divided the people, and – unlike the usual, 'politically correct' impression spread by the media – in a very different fashion to the 'usual', much acclaimed national, ethnic, and religious lines. Similarly, contemporary political propaganda, and also professional commentators and interested third parties, at home and abroad, were all insisting on putting all the blame for the conflict that destroyed the Socialist Federative Republic of Yugoslavia (Socialistička Federativna Republika Jugoslavia, SFRJ) on the 'other side'; on painting a 'black and white' picture of this war.

The reality was – and remains – significantly different. It starts with the fact that none of the members of the Yugoslav Air Force and Air Defence Force (Ratno vazduhoplovstvo i protivvazdušna Odbrana, RV i PVO, colloquially 'JRV i PVO') I know about could have predicted the war, and then could have predicted the way it would end. The process initiated by nearly all of the involved politicians was de-facto invisible to all of us wearing the uniform: generally, we were convinced we would be fighting to preserve the SFRJ, and had no doubts about the outcome. That is why members of all nationalities continued to serve regardless the circumstances, why they flew combat sorties throughout the summer and autumn of 1991, and then the winter of 1991-1992. In this regard, things began to change only in the first half of 1992: only then was the RV i PVO to receive a predominantly Serbian and Montenegrin character.

This project came into being in the course of intensive, every-day research over the last 30 years: a research that became my profession, and research that is never going to end. While collecting thousands of documents and other kind of materials, my only problem – and the biggest fear of all those providing me with information – were possible repercussions related to their participation in these events: very strong political propaganda remains omni-present, severe pressure is exercised upon nearly all participants and eyewitnesses, and criminal proceedings are initiated by the International Criminal Tribunal for the former Yugoslavia (ICTY) in Den Haag, often for entirely incomprehensible reasons. Perhaps the most absurd example was the prosecution of a retired pilot of Serbian nationality nowadays living in Belgrade, for flying in the rear seat of a Mikoyan i Gurevich MiG-21UM two-seat conversion trainer: in the front seat was a Croat who had decided not to fire unguided rockets and returned the aircraft to base with both launchers still full. In autumn 1991, that pilot went to the Croatian Air Force (Hrvatsko ratno zrakoplovstvo i protuzračna obrana, HRZ i PZO), while – at the request of the Croatian judicial system – his former colleague was interrogated by the Serbian police,

16 years later, in 2007. What a surprise then, when the mass of participants prefers to remain silent until this very day.

Although millions of photographs had been taken in 1991-1992, good photographs remain a rarity. No doubt, the activities of the RV i PVO were recorded by the internal service magazine *Krila Armije*. However, the last issue of the same was published for the Day of the RV i PVO, on 21 May 1991. Coincidentally, I was a soldier in the position of a journalist of the *Krila Armije*, and acting within well-established service rules, but there were few opportunities for taking photographs. Another problem was that at the time the RV i PVO was dominated by enthusiasm for the highly-popular video cameras in the VHS format: tragically, all the resulting material disappeared without a trace. That is why finding any good photograph from that period is a great discovery.

I would like to express my gratitude for all the assistance to my superior from 1991 and 1992, editor of *Krila Armije* Major (retired) Mladen Savić, who tried to record the events in the first months of the war with a photo camera. I would like to forward my thanks to Zdenko Molnar, a non-commissioned officer (NCO) and a photographer in the command of the air force in 1991; to Zoran Milovanović from the Photo Centre of the Yugoslav National Army (Jugoslovenska narodna armija, JNA; this Photo Centre is nowadays the Media Centre of *Odbrana* magazine); to Milorad Ristić from the Aeronautical Museum in Surčin; to Srđan Ilić, one of the best war photographers ever; to a paratrooper and modeller Boško Čeliković; to the former Chief of Aeronautical Museum Lieutenant Colonel (ret.) Predrag Grandić, to Tomaž Perme for assistance in collecting material on the conflict in Slovenia and Josip Novak and Nenad Šetina for photographs from the war in Croatia and to many others who helped collect the material. I owe a great deal of gratitude for the translation from Serbian language into English language to my friend Ivan Luković.

From the Second World War until 1980 the top executive powers in Yugoslavia were in the hands of Marshal Josip Broz Tito, a charismatic leader who skilfully maintained balance in interethnic relations. Tito was ideologized in the form of a strong personality cult in the JNA, demonstrated during his official visits to specific units: at Batajnica AB in 1975, he wore an air force uniform and hat. Tito proudly posed for photographers and one of the resulting pictures was then distributed to the walls and desks of the offices of the RV i PVO. When the civil war in Yugoslavia erupted, most of the photos were quickly discarded and ended up in dumps. (RV i PVO)

1 BACKGROUND AND CONTEXT

The idea of linking the South Slavic peoples of the Balkans into a single state emerged in the 14th century on the wave of the broader pan-Slavic movement. Romantic nationalist emotions were not sufficient for the accomplishment of the plan, but the fall of the Austro-Hungarian Empire opened the way to the emergence of new states. On 1 December 1918, the Kingdom of Serbs, Croats, and Slovenians (SHS) was established. This consisted of Serbia – which fought in the First World War on the side of the Entente – and parts of the Austro-Hungarian Empire, which fell apart at the end of that conflict. Six days after, and on order from the Prince Regent Aleksandar I Karađorđevic of Serbia, the Supreme Command of the armed forces of the new state issued the order for the Serbian Army to take control of the territory of the new state as soon as possible due to the unstable political situation and unspecified borders. In December 1918, flying units of the Serbian Army were deployed in Novi Sad, under French control: other units were formed within the present day Croatia and Slovenia from whatever was left of the Austro-Hungarian Air Force: on 26 June, Regent Aleksandar (crowned king in 1921), issued a decree under which an Air Force Command was established at a brigade level, directly subordinated to the Engineering and Technical Administration of the Ministry of the Army. Under often confusing circumstances, combat aircraft of these units had participated in the fighting on the northern border of the new state, against Austria, but also on the border with Hungary – affected by a communist revolution – and in operations against an Albanian insurgency in the south.[1]

The air force of the SHS was thus consolidated 'on the move': initially, it primarily consisted of Serbian veterans from the Thessaloniki front of the First World War, and a few of their former enemies that had served with the air force of the Austro-Hungarian Monarchy. In August 1920, the Administration of the Air Force was established, and the first modernisation was initiated with support from France. Correspondingly, the new service was re-equipped with Breguet 19 and 25 biplanes manufactured under licence, and Dewoitine D.I and D.9 fighters. In 1921, the Naval Aviation came into being: this was initially equipped with indigenous IO reconnaissance aircraft, and IM trainers, but later re-equipped with German-made Dornier Do.Ds. By 1923, the first commander of the nascent air force (and the last commander of the Austro-Hungarian air force), General Milan Uzelac (an ethnic Serb born in Komarno in modern-day Slovakia), not only reorganised his service, but also initiated the launch of the local aviation industry. In 1927, the Air Force Command was elevated to the army level, as a separate branch of the armed forces equal to the Army and the Navy.

Royal Yugoslav Army Air Force

When King Aleksandar I caused a political crisis in the SHS by establishing himself as dictator, in January 1929, he changed the official designation of the country into Kraljevina Jugoslavija (Kingdom of Yugoslavia). Correspondingly, the air force received the official designation of the Royal Yugoslav Air Force. Henceforth, official policies insisted on strengthening Yugoslav nationality and related feelings. In turn, Aleksandar was assassinated by Croat nationalists on 1 October 1934. During these five years, the entire country and thus its air force were severely shaken by the global economic crisis, which postponed further modernisation for several years. Thus, it still flew mostly locally manufactured variants of various French designs, Czechoslovak-made Avia BH.33Es, and British-made Hawker Furies. It was only in 1936, that a major modernization was launched, prompted by a realistic assessment that a large new war was looming. Aircraft were procured from all sides and that is why Yugoslav squadrons had technology originating from counties that would fight against each other during the Second World War. British-made Bristol Blenheim Mk I light bombers and Hawker Hurricane Mk I fighters served alongside the German-made Dornier Do-17K bombers manufactured under license. The backbone of the fighter-fleet was made of Messerschmitt Bf.109E-3 interceptors of German origin; Italian-made Savoia-Marchetti SM.79 bombers formed most of the bomber-fleet, while domestic Ikarus IK-3 fighters were also in production. In the course of this reorganisation, the air force was established as a separate branch of the military and received blue uniforms.

On 25 March 1941 Yugoslavia joined the German-Italian military alliance, but two days later a coup led by officers of the air force toppled the government. The commander of the air force, General Dušan Simović, became the Prime Minister and King Petar II Karađorđević, at that time a minor, was crowned. The reaction of the Axis was swift: on 6 April 1941 its forces commenced an attack on Yugoslavia and Greece with 83 divisions and 2,236 aircraft. In defence, the Yugoslav air force had around 1,000 various aircraft (including about 330 modern combat types), and around 50,000 officers and other ranks. The Axis forces quickly proved to be superior and the Yugoslav resistance collapsed in a matter of only a few days. One squadron of naval aviation flew over around 2,000 kilometres down the Adriatic Sea and across the Mediterranean Sea to Abu Qir, in Egypt, to join the

A map of the administrative and political organisation of the SFRJ, with native and English names of all of its six Federal Republics, and the two autonomous provinces in Serbia. (Map by Tom Cooper)

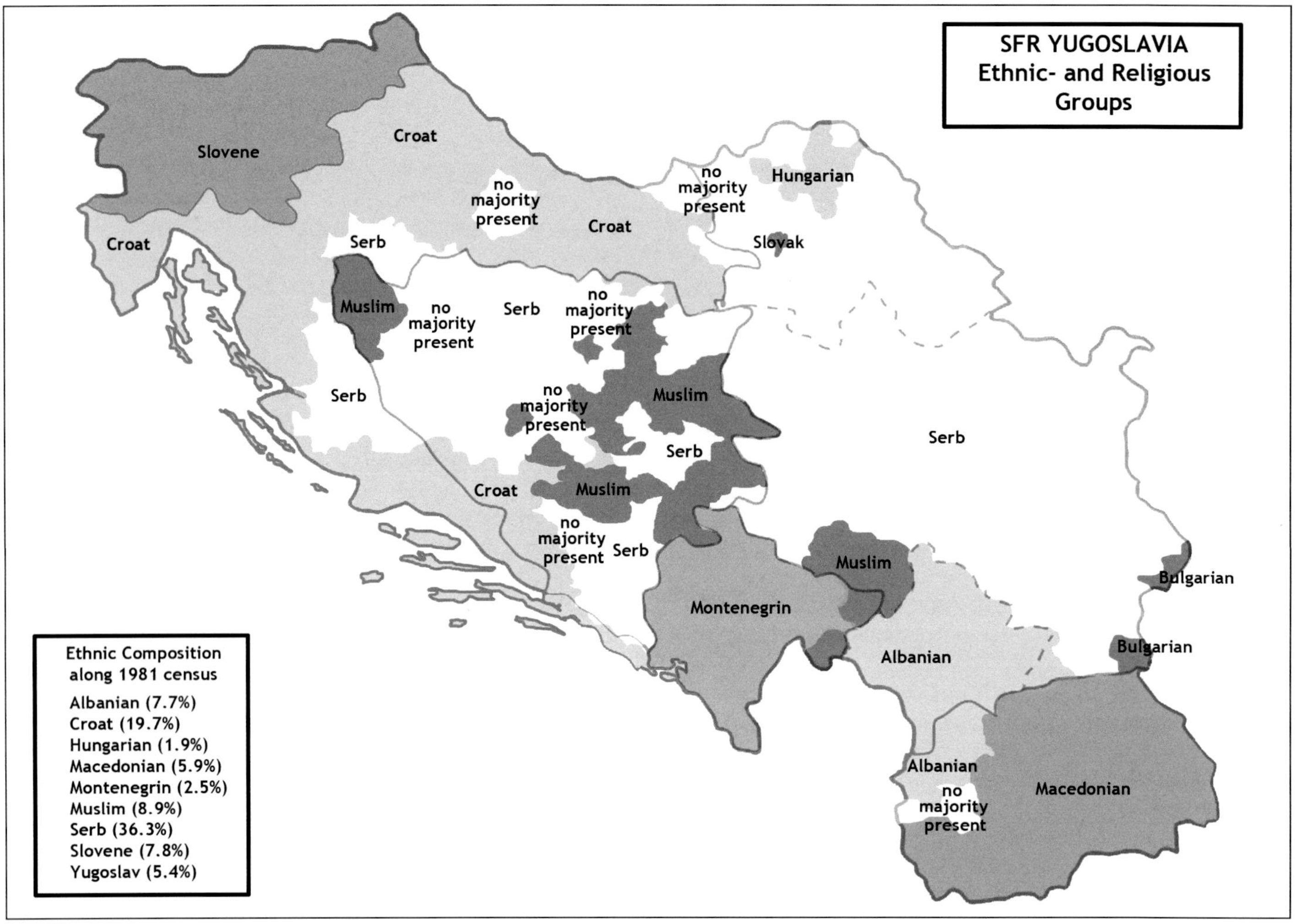

Based on the data from the 1981 census, this map shows just how diverse the composition of ethnic and religious groups of the SFRJ was – especially within the geographic centres of the country, in Bosnia and Herzegovina, and in Croatia. The complexity of the Yugoslav Crisis was based on a national structure that did not correspond to the borders of Federal units – which is why the causes and the course of this conflict cannot be understood without a view of the ethnic and religious composition of the population. (Map by Tom Cooper)

Royal Air Force (RAF). Dozens of pilots from other units defected in various ways and also joined the RAF. Meanwhile, the Axis powers and their allies in Hungary and Bulgaria divided Yugoslavia into several zones under control of the German, Italian, Bulgarian, and Hungarian forces, and Croat and Serbian collaborators.

The Second World War and the resurrected Yugoslav Air Force

During the summer of 1941, an insurgency against the Axis forces erupted, led by two major mutually-hostile parties from opposite sides of the ideological spectrum: the 'Partisans' were led by Josip Broz Tito and the Communist Party, while the 'Četniks' (Chetniks) initially waged an anti-Croat and anti-Axis insurgency, but eventually turned against the leftists and their allies and fought one another in a bitter civil war. Simultaneously, the pro-Axis government of Croatia organised its own air force, a large segment of which took part in the invasion of the Union of the Soviet Socialist Republics (USSR/Soviet Union) as a part of the German Luftwaffe under the designation Croatian Air Force Legion (Kroatische Luftwaffen-Legion). Consisting of one bomber squadron and one fighter squadron, these operated on the Eastern Front as the 10th, later 15th Squadron of Bomber Wing 53, and the 15th Squadron of Fighter Wing 52 (originally III./JG.52, later 15(Kroat.)/JG.52), respectively, from 1941 until 1944.

Meanwhile, on 23 May 1942, the Partisans symbolically established their own air force when three members of the Croatian air force defected to their side flying obsolete Potez 19 and Breguet 19 biplanes. However, this guerrilla aviation was short-lived. In its place, and with British support, a core of the future air force came into being through the establishment of No. 351 Squadron RAF (equipped with Hurricane Mk. IVs) and No. 352 Squadron (equipped with Spitfire Mk. Vs) in 1944. Worked up in Libya, the two units initially operated from air bases in Italy, before a few Spitfires were re-deployed to the liberated island of Vis in October 1944. Matching the British support, in early 1945, the Soviets handed over the complement of an entire attack division equipped with Ilyushin Il-2 close air support (CAS) fighters and one fighter division equipped with Yakovlev Yak-1 and Yak-3s to Tito's Partisans, who were meanwhile in charge of most of the country that was ultimately (in 1963) re-named to the SFRJ. Indeed, with Soviet help a new flying branch – the Yugoslav Air Force – was officially established in December 1945. Modelled along the principles of the Soviet Air Force (Voyenno-Vozdushnye Sily, VVS), it included a total of 677 aircraft organised into 40 squadrons. Most of its equipment was of Soviet origin, but additional aircraft were subsequently received from Bulgaria, which had to reduce its arms and pay war reparations under the terms of the peace treaty. Correspondingly, during the late 1940s, the JRV received 50 Messerschmitt Bf.109Gs and additional Il-2s and also Petyakov Pe-2FT bombers, Yak-3, and Yak-9P interceptors.

Informburo Period

Unlike other counties of eastern Europe that ended up under Soviet dominance, a strong drive for complete independence existed in the post-Second World War Yugoslavia, and the new government was

In the background of this photo of a MiG-21M from 130th Fighter Aviation Squadron are the peaks of the Šar Mountains, which was a landmark for pilots from Priština, an air base located in the central part of Kosovo, a region in which political demonstrations by ethnic Albanians were launched repeatedly during the 1980s. (Siniša Šijačić)

determined to rely on its own armed forces. Correspondingly, the aviation industry was rebuilt and serial production of piston-engined trainers initiated, while on the diplomatic front Yugoslavia established close ties with Albania and Bulgaria. When the rift between Belgrade and Moscow became obvious, in late June 1948 the Soviets addressed the Yugoslav people with a call to overturn their government: Tito's Communists managed to retain control and consolidate their political situation, nevertheless and the USSR and its East-European-allies threatened an invasion. All of a sudden, former allies turned into major enemies that blocked their borders, shot at – and killed – Yugoslav border guards, and repeatedly violated the Yugoslav airspace.

Under pressure from what subsequently developed into the Warsaw Pact – the Soviet-dominated defence pact controlling all of Eastern Europe – the Yugoslavs rapidly reorganised and re-deployed much of their air force to the western parts of the country. At the beginning of this crisis – known in Yugoslavia as the Informburo Period – the RV i PVO had only 96 Yak-3, Yak-9, and Yak-9P interceptors.[2] Correspondingly, in 1949 the Yugoslavs launched the production of their indigenous equivalent, the Ikarus S-49A: this was based on technical documentation and research for the IK-3 from 1938-1939, and adapted to be powered by the Soviet-made VK-104 engine. Only a year later, no less than 46 S-49As were available for the defence of Belgrade.

As the Cold War heated up, the government of the United States of America (USA) began searching for additional allies. Recognising that the Yugoslavs had distanced themselves from the USSR, they seized the opportunity and in 1951 signed the Mutual Defense Aid Program (MDAP) – originally intended only to rebuild the conventional militaries of the North Atlantic Treaty Organisation (NATO) – under which Yugoslavia was granted permission to receive extensive amounts of US-made armament and equipment. Because of the continuous crisis between Belgrade and Moscow, the Americans rushed to reinforce the RV i PVO through shipments of British-made de Havilland Mosquito and US-made Republic P-47D Thunderbolt fighter-bombers. The next step was jets, and in March 1953 the first Lockheed T-33A arrived at Batajnica AB outside Belgrade. The Americans continued supporting communist-dominated Yugoslavia and in 1958 provided the first shipment of Republic F-84G Thunderjet fighter-bombers, followed by RT-33A reconnaissance fighters, and then North American F-86E Sabre interceptors. Although the procurement through the MDAP ceased in the same year, the Yugoslavs then continued buying US-made aircraft through commercial contracts most of which were supported by Washington, which granted favourable conditions. For example, in 1961 and 1962, they purchased North American F-86D Sabre Dog fighters and Lockheed TV-2 jet trainers (the latter were a variant of the T-33A manufactured for the US Navy). Meanwhile, the domestic aviation industry continued manufacturing various trainers and Ikarus S-49C advanced piston-engined interceptors.

Drvar-1 and Drvar-2

From 1950, the JNA and the RV i PVO were completely reorganised with the aim of converting them from the traditions of guerrilla warfare during the Second World War to defence against a sudden and massive aggression supported by nuclear weapons. The peak of this process was reached in 1959-1961, when the armed forces were reorganised under Plan Drvar-1, and the air force received its ultimate official designation: the RV i PVO. Only three years later, Plan Drvar-2 re-shaped its structure once again, and then through organising it into two air corps. As relations with the USSR normalised, in 1961 Yugoslavia began buying Soviet-made armament again. Correspondingly, by 1965, the RV i PVO acquired Mikoyan i Gurevich MiG-21F-13 interceptors (ASCC/NATO-codename 'Fishbed'), a regiment of SA-75M Dvina surface-to-air missiles (SAMs, ASCC/NATO-codename 'SA-2b Guideline Mod 1'), and Soviet-made P-30 early warning radars (ASCC/NATO-codename 'Big Mesh'). Subsequently, it continued to purchase advanced versions of most of these systems, including MiG-21PFMs, MiG-21M/MFs and MiG-21bis, as well as Volkhov (ASCC/NATO-codename 'SA-2d Guideline Mod 3) and Neva-M (ASCC/NATO-codename 'SA-3b Goa Mod 1') SAMs. Moreover, in 1966, the two corps of the RV i PVO were re-organised as two air defence divisions that – following the example of the VVS – included units equipped with manned fighters, units equipped with surface-to-air missiles (SAMs), and units equipped for aerial surveillance. On the contrary, the domestic aviation industry firmly anchored itself to the technical footing of the West. From 1958 the Aeronautical Technical Institute (VTI), in the Belgrade neighbourhood of Žarkovo was established: this led to the development of what eventually entered operational service as the Soko Galeb-2 training aircraft and the Soko J-21 Jastreb light striker, powered by British-made Rolls-Royce Viper turbojets, equipped with British and French-made avionics, and manufactured by a factory in Mostar. The reliance on Western technology was obvious during the research and development of the second generation of Yugoslav Jets, including the Soko J-22 Orao and the Soko Galeb-4.[3]

The Warsaw Pact`s invasion of Czechoslovakia in 1968 left a strong impression on the JNA. A new position was reinforced that procurement of armaments should be diversified to several sources and that investments should be made into the domestic defence industry as an independent source of supply. Then, the armed forces were formed from two elements – the JNA and the reservist Territorial Defence (Teritorijalna odbrana, TO): the former was a part of the Federal authorities under the jurisdiction of the Federal Secretariat of People's Defence (Savezni sekretarijat za narodnu odbranu, SSNO), in the communist era an equivalent of the Ministry of Defence. The activities of the TO were under the jurisdiction of the constituent republics, each of which had its own Secretariat of People's Defence – the HQ of the TO. In wartime, it was foreseen that the JNA and TO would create unified armed forces. In peacetime influences from the federal level intertwined with the interests of the leadership of Federal units, which demanded that the national cadre must lead the TO. Because the JNA consisted of three services – ground forces (Kopnena vojska, KoV), air force and air defence (RV i PVO), and a navy (Ratna mornarica, RM) – the equivalents of all three services were formed in the TO, even if this primarily consisted of ground units. According to the war plans aviation squadrons and flights were formed within the TO, using aircraft drawn from civilian aviation, flown by reserve pilots and maintained by reservist ground personnel.

Beginning of the End: Kosovo of 1981

Following the death of the Yugoslav leader Tito in 1980, foreign observers expected a deep crisis in the inter-ethnic relations of the SFRJ and assessed this as likely to destroy the country within a few years at most. As time was to show, this process was to take longer than expected. Nevertheless, an inter-ethnic crisis did develop in Kosovo and Metohija, then an autonomous province in southern Serbia, colloquially known as the 'Kosmet'.

The uprising was initially sparked amongst Albanian students at Priština University on 11 March 1981, and the reason might appear 'trivial': they complained about the poor quality of the food in the local cantina. Correspondingly, their message was of local and social nature and also coloured by Marxist-Leninist ideology. However, the longer the protests went on, the more nationalist the character and stronger the political message became. Eventually, the protesters began chanting, 'We are Albanians, no Yugoslavs!' Indeed, before long, hundreds of thousands of people took to the streets of towns in the Kosmet and demonstrations culminated on 26 March 1981, when the local police ('Milicija', frequently – yet wrongly – translated as 'militia', although it was a professional service responsible for maintaining civilian law and order), attempted to break them up. Lacking sufficient anti-riot assets, it failed, and on 2 April 1981, the Presidency of the SFRJ not only declared a state of emergency, but significantly reinforced the local police, and then a military intervention.

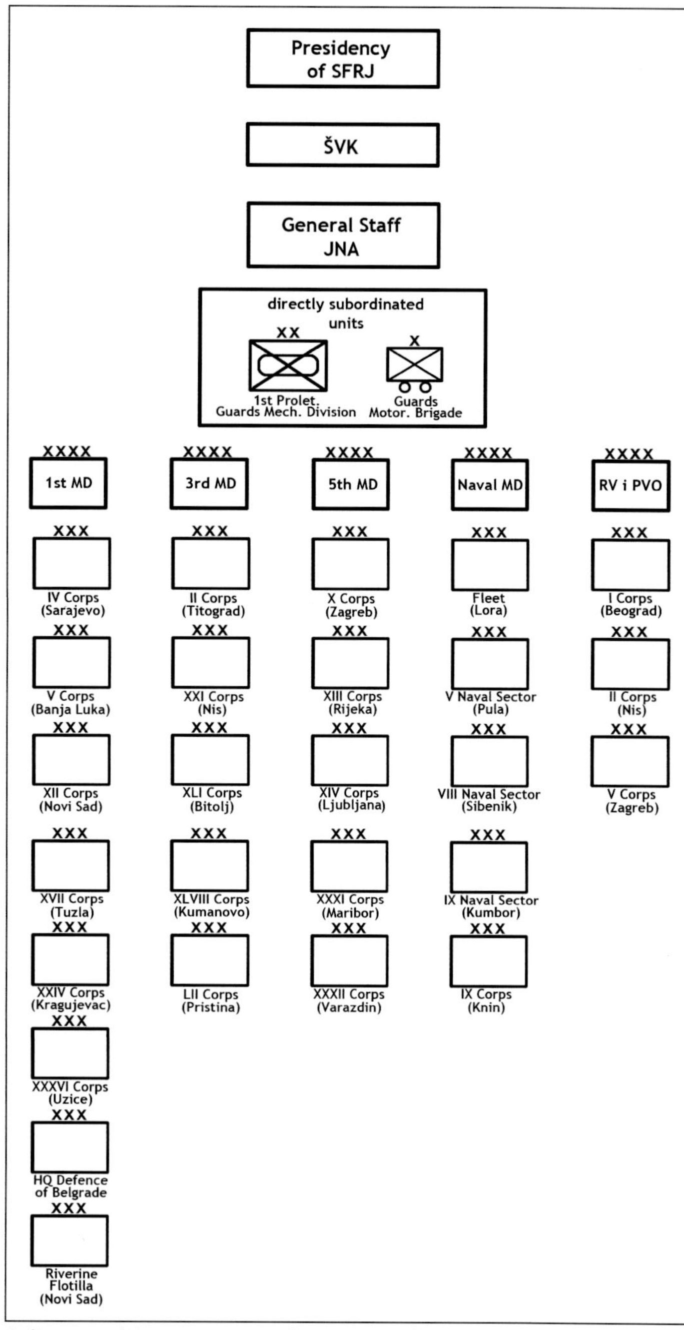

A diagram of the top command structures of the JNA (and the RV i PVO) under Plan Jedinstvo, realised during the second half of the 1980s. Notably, X Corps with HQ in Zagreb was established only in 1990. (Diagram by Tom Cooper)

The JNA thus not only deployed units of the locally-based LII Corps on the streets of all the major towns, but also brought in reinforcements from garrisons in Macedonia and central Serbia to provide direct support and protect vital infrastructure. Indeed, assessing that major military bases required special protection measures, the JNA deployed the entire 211th Armoured Brigade from Niš to guard the Slatina AB, outside Priština, which housed the MiG-21s of the 83rd Fighter Aviation Regiment (FAR). That said, the RV i PVO took little part in calming down the crisis, except for flying transport and liaison missions. A pair of its Soviet-made Mil Mi-8 helicopters was re-painted from their usual olive-drab overall to blue-white, to mimic police operations: after all, the survival of Yugoslavia was heavily dependent upon good relations between its diverse ethnic and religious groups – defined by the official policy of 'Brotherhood and Unity' ('bratstvo i jedinstvo'), but was also dependent upon income from tourism, and thus the government in Belgrade was very keen to maintain a positive public image.

Fading Unity

What did shatter the fundaments of the SFRJ of the 1980s was a major economic crisis. Caused by a very rapid economic growth in the 1970s financed by reckless borrowing abroad, this over-extended the economy and resulted in a massive debt load of US$21 billion. A combination of incompetence, corruption, and inability to serve foreign debts then caused a hyper-inflation at a time when Western creditors proved unwilling to generously restructure Yugoslavia's debts as tensions with the USSR began lessening following Mikhail Gorbachev become a leader in Moscow. As the crisis went on for years without any sign of an improvement (average real earnings decreased by 25 percent between 1975 and 1985), additional and ever larger corruption scandals were uncovered, causing the ordinary people to lose the faith in the competence and honesty of the country's communist leadership. Eventually, massive rifts between constituent republics emerged as the two wealthier western republics, Slovenia and Croatia, felt they were paying too much into the Federal budget, while Serbia demanded that they pay more. This re-focused the politics along the traditional fault line within Yugoslavia – the one between the Croats and the Serbs.

Heavily politicised, the leadership of the armed forces continued insisting on the status quo and continued with 'business as usual'. Indeed, having a strong political and propaganda message, the word 'unity' ('jedinstvo') was selected for the next major reorganisation of the JNA – and thus the RV i PVO – in the mid-1980s: Plan Jedinstvo. This aimed to address the threat of increasingly independent political leaderships of diverse Federal units, which could easily prove fatal for the future of the SFRJ. The reason was that as a result of the decision to create the Territorial Defence forces, each of the six republics of the federation had its own armed forces. Adapted by the government and the JNA in 1982, Plan Jedinstvo saw the reorganisation of traditional strategic zones of the country's defence into four 'areas of responsibility' (AoRs): the north-west, central, south-east and the military naval zone. In peace-time, these served as 'military districts', whose AoRs overlapped administrative borders of the six republics. Under Plan Jedinstvo, and in the case of an emergency, all the units within any of the theatres of war/military districts – regardless if those of the JNA or the TO – were to be subjected to the overall control of the JNA. In this way, the armed forces also expected to prevent the destruction of the SFRJ from within.

From the point of view of the RV i PVO, Plan Jedinstvo was adopted in 1986, when all of its units were subjected to the control of three air force and air defence corps – envisaged as joint operational units for territorial air defence and for air support of one or more groups of land forces, naval forces, and the TO in the specific theatre of operations, in both defensive and offensive operations. The three corps of the RV i PVO were as follows:

- I Corps, HQ Belgrade, responsible for the Adriatic coast and central Yugoslavia
- III Corps, HQ Niš, responsible for south-eastern Yugoslavia
- V Corps, HQ Zagreb, was responsible for north-western Yugoslavia

A large exercise, Jedinstvo-83, held from 25 August to 11 October 1983, with the focus on the region of central and eastern Macedonia, was a message to the Albanians on the strength of the JNA. T-72M tanks that were procured from the USSR in 1981 were seen in public for the first time. (Media Center Odbrana)

The conventional scenario of the Cold War-era dominated exercise Jedinstvo-83 – mass attacks of tanks were shown with the support of the artillery and aviation, however the intervention of police in one of the cities was the realistic future of the SFRJ. A Macedonian police unit demonstrated the destruction of terrorists with the support of a TAB-71 APC (a Romanian version of the Soviet BTR-60). (Media Center Odbrana)

During exercise Deneb-89, 172nd Fighter-Bomber Avioation Regiment flew over from Golubovci AB to Udbina AB, an airfield of the so-called B category in the region of Lika which during peacetime had no units of the RV i PVO. Both squadrons from 172nd FBAR, with 13 Galeb-4 and 13 NJ-21 and J-21 Jastrebs took part in the largest exercise in the 1980s. (Krila armije)

Obviously, the structure of each of the three of air force's corps varied, depending on its geographic area of responsibility and possible tasks. However, in principle, each was in control of several brigades, regiments, bases and battalions, with the following purposes:

- one or more of the aviation brigades served the purpose of reconnaissance, air defence, and ground or naval attack
- one aviation brigade served the purpose of transport and casualty evacuation
- one FAR served the purpose of intercepting and destroying airborne targets, with reconnaissance as its secondary role
- multiple air defence units (some brigade-sized, others regiment-sized), with the purpose of air defence of specific areas or installations of strategic importance, or groups of ground forces, and the sealing of important flight routes of aviation and unmanned aerial vehicles
- one air surveillance regiment serving the purpose of detection, early warning, and command and control (through provision of the command post for the corps in question)
- multiple air bases, the purpose of which was provision of logistics and combat security services to the flying aviation
- multiple signal battalions, engineer battalions and at least one battalion for electronic intelligence (ELINT) gathering purposes

The bulk of the JNA was reorganised under Plan Jedinstvo in 1988 and 1989. Designations of its three Military Districts were identical to those the RV i PVO:

- 1st Military District (MD): Central Yugoslavia
- 3rd MD: south-east Yugoslavia
- 5th MD: north-west Yugoslavia

One exception to this rule was the Naval District, which exercised command and control over both the Yugoslav Navy and also ground forces deployed along the Adriatic coast, foremost in Dalmatia – the southernmost part of Croatia – and in Montenegro.

As a result of this reorganisation, and to emphasise the unity of command and the force (the land forces, the RV i PVO, the Navy,

In 1991, the real political power in SFRJ was in the hands of six national leaders of its constituent republics: from left to right are Momir Bulatović (Montenegro), Alija Izetbegović (Bosnia-Herzegovina), Slobodan Milošević (Serbia), Kiro Gligorov (Macedonia), Franjo Tuđman (Croatia) and Milan Kučan (Slovenia). (Vojkan Kostić collection)

and the TO), the General Staff of the JNA was re-designated as the General Staff of the Armed Forces of the SFRJ. At the operational level, all Army-level commands were disbanded: in their place a corps-structure came into being, the headquarters of which was directly subordinated to the command of every MD. Similarly, all the divisions were disbanded, and the ground forces switched over to the brigade-model. Further down the chain of the command, all the TO units were subordinated to the HQs of the MDs, while the staff of the TO-zones was supposed to be subjected to the control of every corps. Moreover, the General Staff had developed two new major war plans that were to prove crucial for the future function of the entire armed forces:

- Plan Sutjeska-1 envisaged an invasion by the Warsaw Pact from the east
- Plan Sutjeska-2 envisaged an invasion by NATO from the west

Due to the complexity of internal relations in the country, it was understood that the aggressor would lean on the so-called 'internal enemy' nationalists and opponents of the socialist political order, but the later were not expected to play an important role in the overall context.

On 24 February 1989, two police air unit AB.212s transported 13 members of the Serbia's Police Unit for Special Actions (Jedinica milicije za specijalna dejstva), from their base at the international airport Belgrade to the military barracks in Kosovska Mitrovica. On the evening of 27 February, they received the approval for raid actions against Albanian strikers in the depths of the Stari Trg coal mine. This photograph is from one of the exercises of the unit in the mid-1980s. (Serbia's Ministry of the Interior)

In clashes with Albanian demonstrators, on 27 March 1989, anti-riot units deployed TAB-71 APCs. The clashes were serious and TV stations showed clips of shots being fired from the turret-mounted 14.5mm machinegun of an APC. (Srđan Ilić)

War Plans and Exercises

Between 1986 and 1988, the new organisation and function of the three newly-formed corps of the RV i PVO were put to the test and further honed in the course of one large command post-level exercise, and multiple joint tactical exercises – of which the later also saw the participation of ground and naval forces. The first such exercise was Sava-86, held in 1986 within the zone of responsibility of V Corps, in north-western Yugoslavia. A year later, Vardar-87 was run by III Corps, and in 1988 Dunav-88 by I Corps. For Yugoslav conditions, these were major operations: for example, no less than 9,649 officers and other ranks, 192 fixed-wing and 26 rotor-wing aircraft, 59 radar systems, 547 anti-aircraft guns, 60 launchers for man-portable air defence missiles – all Soviet-made Strela-1M (ASCC/NATO-codename 'SA-9 Gaskin Mod 1'), and Strela-2M (ASCC/NATO-codename 'SA-7b Grail') MANPADS – 20 battalions of S-125 Neva-M and 2K12 Kub-M (ASCC/NATO-codename 'SA-6 Gainful') SAMs were deployed during Dunav-88 alone.

The primary focus in each of these exercises was to test the new, dual-purpose structure of air defence and air-support tasks. All the scenarios were based on the idea that the initial aggression would be initiated by a superior opponent, simultaneously with a culmination of an internal conflict. For example, Dunav-88 began with the assumption that the aggressor (always called the 'blue force') would launch an offensive including 2,000 combat aircraft, surface-to-surface missiles and widespread commando operations, which caused heavy destruction to the infrastructure and military industry. The internal enemies then became active in all parts of Yugoslavia, but particularly in Kosovo i Metohija – an autonomous province in southern Serbia, colloquially known as the 'Kosmet': indeed, there the General Staff expected the insurgency to cooperate directly with the Albanian

In 1989, Mi-8s from the Niš-based 119th Aviation Brigade, in a blue and white scheme, were used to support the police and armed forces in Kosovo. Instead of the air force's serial, they had a civilian registration YU-HCD, under which one police AB.212 helicopter had been registered. To differentiate them, the Mi-8s used serials YU-HCD-1 and YU-HCD-2. (Krila Armije)

Army. In similar fashion, any 'democratic/pluralist' leadership of any of the Federal Republics was expected to openly side with the 'blue force', i.e. with the 'bad' side. The defender (always called the 'red force'), was expected to suffer heavy losses early on, then withdraw to reorganise and rearm before striking back. For example, the scenario for Dunav-88 envisaged wing-sized air strikes by NATO, followed by the occupation of Sarajevo and Belgrade, where new 'quisling' governments would be established. The Warsaw Pact had carried out a partial mobilization, and the governments of its members condemned the aggression, but limited themselves to supporting the 'reds' with arms and ammunition only.

However, the biggest joint tactical exercise of this period was Deneb-89.[4] Held from 27 to 31 May 1989 and based on the idea of a NATO offensive into western Yugoslavia, this for the first time ever saw the RV i PVO operating as an independent branch of the armed forces. Indeed, in this scenario, following the opening invasion of the 'blue force', supported by 5th Allied Tactical Air Force (5th ATAF) of NATO in Italy, and two aircraft carriers deployed in the Adriatic roughly between Ancona and Zadar, friendly ground forces withdrew before settling down for the defence. A squadron drawn from V Corps RV i PVO simulated the 'blue', while the 'red force' was drawn from squadrons of the I Corps. In the course of this exercise, the red force launched its own counteroffensive with the aim of breaking the aerial dominance of the enemy over western Yugoslavia. Correspondingly, during Deneb-89, many units of the RV i PVO were forward deployed along the Adriatic coast and on 29 May 1989 they held a live-firing exercise on the Tramerka Range (off the coast of Zadar), targeting simulated NATO aircraft and ships.

Explosion of Nationalism

Meanwhile, a growing number of political leaders of all six republics of the SFRJ began fostering nationalism, forming the basis for a future armed conflict. Preservation of 'brotherhood and unity' – indeed: of the entire SFRJ – was quickly swept under the carpet while local political leaders, and the media supporting them, launched propaganda campaigns aimed at creating an atmosphere of consolidation along ethnic lines, and mutual distrust and confrontation between the Serbs, Croats and Slovenes. Before long, even communist leaders of the two westernmost Federal Republics – Slovenia and Croatia – began publicly propagating a loose confederation, while actually aiming for independence. Serbia was no exception: originally a staunch communist, the leader of the local branch of the communist party and president of the Federal Republic, Slobodan Milošević turned into a populist encouraging the nationalist sentiments, even if – hypocritically – 'demanding preservation of the SFRJ.' Declaring strict centralisation as an answer to the incompetence and corruption of the federal system, in 1988 and 1989, Milošević exploited his popularity to run a series of coups that ousted his rivals in Serbia, Vojvodina, Kosmet, and then in Montenegro, thus establishing him in a dominant position within the collective eight-member presidency of the entire SFRJ. What had once been the pro-Yugoslav and muli-national current that flowed throughout the political life of Yugoslavia disappeared between 1988 and 1991.

Renewed Albanian Demonstrations

Once again, the spark that caused the ultimate show-down was delivered by the Albanians in the Kosmet. In early 1989, multiple amendments for the Constitution of Serbia were announced, including a limitation of the autonomy of its two provinces – Vojvodina, in the north, and the Kosmet in the south. On 20 February 1989, miners of the Stari Trg zinc mine, almost exclusively ethnic Albanians, went on strike. The authorities took this escalation seriously and deployed the Special Operations Police Unit during the night of 27 to 28 February. The operators descended 850-metres-deep through the vent-shafts to take the miners by surprise and overpower their guards: by the morning, the strike was broken and all 50 workers were on the surface.

Meanwhile, on 27 February 1989, a state of emergency in the Kosmet was declared again, and the Presidency of the SFRJ ordered the deployment of security forces. Once again, the JNA deployed in support of the police, primarily with tanks and armoured vehicles used for the protection of vital installations, but also as a power demonstration. Finally, under severe pressure from Belgrade, the Parliament of the Autonomous Province of Kosovo i Metohija adopted constitutional amendments and reduced the autonomy of the province. On the same day, mass demonstrations erupted and continued during the following night and into the morning. The rioters ransacked the police station in Podujevo, killing the chief of the station. Eventually, the police responded with firearms and two people – including another officer – were killed. In attempt to restore order, the police established a Joint Detachment, grouping special-purpose units from all over the SFRJ. However, its raids and other measures failed to suppress the unrest and by early 1990 protesters were back on the streets of Kosovo. Eventually, the Presidency decided to introduce additional – drastic – methods and end the emergency once and for all.

During the unrests in Kosovo the RV i PVO units stationed within the province were put on different levels of combat readiness as a measure to protect their bases, equipment and people. Units equipped with Mi-8s and Aérospatiale SA.341H and SA.342L Gazelle helicopters – locally manufactured under licence as the Soko Gazelle – flew transport and liaison sorties, while other units based at Priština and Petrovac made flights at very low altitudes as a show of force and to demonstrate the resolve of the Federal authorities. One of the RV i

PVO MiG-21 pilots assigned to 83rd FAR at the time recalled: 'Despite the high speed of my aircraft, I could clearly see columns of protesters holding candles'.[5]

A direct consequence from the emergency was that all the RV i PVO units began receiving orders to plan their training activities reduced to phraseology like, 'unit XY should achieve top-level readiness for the case of a sudden aggression and emergency'. Unsurprisingly, commanders were left with little choice but to continue preparing their combat operations in the way they were trained throughout the Cold War: under conditions of the enemy deploying strong methods of electronic warfare, nuclear and biological weapons, and for supporting friendly ground forces involved in operations aimed to stem any aggression. Ironically, the Warsaw Pact then dissolved, in late 1989, and Plan Sutjeska-1 lost its purpose. In turn, the JNA and the JRV i PVO thus began heavily concentrating on Plan Sutjeska-2, which envisaged an aggression by NATO, possibly with support of some former Eastern Bloc countries that still had territorial pretensions. On the contrary, while originally an important element of such planning, ethnic- or ideological differences between the diverse peoples of Yugoslavia, were still not considered as a potential threat for stability and security – at least not without being dominated by foreign powers. Indeed, in the shadow of such a position, assessments began emerging within the military leadership that a major coup against the state could be expected from within its own political elites – all of which meanwhile relied on nationalism. It was only late in 1989 that 'democratic ideas' emerged as a big problem for the JNA, because these were considered a 'betrayal' of the ideological values of the Communist Party, to whose control the entire armed forces had been subjected for decades.

Under Plan Radan, from 1988 until 1991, the military police units had priority in regards of replenishment with new personnel. Part of the training of military police in the RV i PVO was firing a standard JNA M70AB2 assault rifle (derivative of Kalashnikov AK-47) from a Mi-8. (Krila Armije)

2

RV i PVO ON THE EVE OF THE WAR

The economic crisis of the 1980s had its impact upon the armed forces. Between 1986 and 1991, the defence budget was decreased from 4.79 percent of the gross domestic product (GDP) to 4 percent. The structure of the budget changed dramatically as ever less was spent to finance procurement: while in 1986, up to 32 percent of the Yugoslav spending for defence was used for acquisition of new or additional armament and equipment, this percentage dropped to 18 percent in 1989, and then 16 percent in 1990. Finally, the senior officers of the JNA could find no other solution than to reorganise its forces once

The 1987 and 1988 acquisition of 16 MiG-29 jets from the USSR opened the beginning of the process of modernisation of the fighter aviation, which until then only had various versions of MiG-21. Unlike most of the counties from the Warsaw Pact and Moscow's clients in the Third World, MiG-23 jets were not used in the SFRJ and a leap was carried out from MiG-21bis to the modern MiG-29. (Aleksandar Radić)

Internal Aircraft Designations of the RV i PVO

In the 1960s, the air force introduced its own system of designating aircraft, based on their type and purpose. While undergoing pre-production testing, locally manufactured aircraft retained their factory name (for example: Galeb and/or Jastreb and similar): once in series production, they would receive a military designation in addition to their original name. The same designation was retained for the aircraft exported abroad. On the other hand, aircraft types purchased from abroad in only small quantities – like Aérospatiale SE.316B Alouette III, Antonov An-2TDs, Canadair CL.215, Dassault Falcon 50s, Dornier Do.27D2, Learjet 25Bs, or Yakovlev Yak-40s – never received any kind of RV i PVO designation.

Table 1: RV i PVO Aircraft Designations	
Factory Designation	**RV i PVO Designation**
L = 'lovac' / fighter (aircraft)	
MiG-21PFM	L-14
MiG-21M/MF	L-15
MiG-21bis	L-17
MiG-21bis-K	L-17K with navigation system ARL-SM Lazur-M
MiG-29	L-18
NL = 'nastavni lovac' / two-seater conversion trainer	
MiG-21U	NL-12
MiG-21US	NL-14
MiG-21UM	NL-16
MiG-29UB	NL-18
I = 'izviđač' / reconnaissance; M = 'modifikovani' / modified	
MiG-21R	L-14i
MiG-21MF with LOROP pod	L-15M
J = 'jurišni' / attack	
Kraguj	J-20
Jastreb J-1	J-21
Orao	J-22
IJ = 'izviđač jurišni' / reconnaissance-attack	
Jastreb RJ-1	IJ-21
Orao	IJ-22
Orao with SLAR pod	INJ-22M
NJ = 'nastavni-jurišni '/ training-attack INJ = 'izviđač-nastavni-jurišni' / reconnaissance-training-attack	
Jastreb TJ	NJ-21
Orao	INJ-22
Orao	NJ-22

again. Thus Plan Jedinstvo-2 and Jedinstvo-3 came into being, which envisaged a gradual reduction in the total troop strength of the JNA by 15 percent. Correspondingly, on 1 January 1990, the RV i PVO had an authorised troop strength of 33,785 officers and other ranks (to be reinforced to 68,552 in wartime).

Finding no other solution out of the economic crisis and the growing political crisis, in March 1989 the SIV was re-organised and received a new president in the form of Ante Marković. A skilled technocrat, Marković reached a new agreement with foreign creditors: in exchange for their patience, he was to reform the entire political system of the SFRJ and hold the first free, multi-party elections since the Second World War, to be held in 1990. Correspondingly, he organised his own party, the Alliance of Reformist Forces, the aim of which was to prove the final attempt to revive Yugoslavia.

Marković's alliance with the JNA was mutually beneficial. However, leading generals remained sceptical about results, and thus carefully monitored the function of the SIV with regards to protecting the SFRJ. Crucial for this process was the function of the Federal Secretary for National Defence, Army-General Veljko Kadijević, a man whose biography reflected the ideology of the entire SFRJ: his father was a

Table 1: RV i PVO Aircraft Designations (*continued*)	
N = nastavni / training	
Galeb G-2A	N-60
Galeb G-2A of a newer series with enhanced avionics	N-60M – 'M' 'modernizovani' / modernized
Galeb G-4	N-62
Galeb G-4 target tug	N-62T – 'T' is tegljač-tug
Lasta	N-63
T = 'transportni' / transport	
Antonov An-26	T-70
V = 'veza' / liaison	
Utva-66	V-51
Utva-75	V-53 – the designation of this aircraft is unusual because it was strictly a trainer
H = 'helikopter' / helicopter	
Mil Mi-8	HT-40
Mi-8 for ELINT	HT-40E – 'E' stood for 'elektronski '/ electronics
SA 341H Gazelle	HO-42 – prefix 'O' stood for 'opšti' / general purpose (utility)
SA 341H Gazelle (search and rescue version)	HS-42 – prefix 'S' stood for 'spasilački' / rescue
SA 341H Gazelle (reconnaissance version, Hera)	Hi-42
SA 341H Gazelle (attack version, Gama)	HN-42M – prefix 'N' stood for 'naoruzani / armed; M for the Gama's basic weapon, Malyutka ATGM
Kamov Ka-25PL	HP-43 – prefix 'P' stood for 'prootivpodmornički' / anti-submarine
Mil Mi-14PL	HP-44
SA 342L Gazelle	HO-45 (most frequently the simplified generic marking H-45 is used in documents)
SA 342L Gazelle in attack version Gama	HN-45M
Kamov Ka-28	HP-46

Table 2: RV i PVO Jet Engine Designations	
Factory/Soviet Designation	**RV i PVO Designation** **MM = 'mlazni motor' / jet engine**
Tumansky R-11F (MiG-21F-13 and MiG-21U)	MM-12
Tumansky R-11F2S-300 (MiG-21PFM, MiG-21R and MiG-21US)	MM-14
Tumansky R-11F2SK-300 (MiG-21M and MiG-21PFM)	MM-15
Tumansky R-13-300 (MiG-21MF, MiG-21M and MiG-21UM)	MM-16
Tumansky R-25-300 (MiG-21bis)	MM-17
Klimov RD-33 (MiG-29 and MiG-29UB)	MM-18

Serb from Dalmatia, in Croatia, and a volunteer of the Spanish Civil War; his mother was a Croat. Kadijević joined Tito's Partisans in 1943 and had a very negative attitude towards nationalism. Moreover, due to its traditional political role and an independent position from that of the leadership of the constituent republics, the JNA was meanwhile known as the 'seventh republic of the SFRJ'. Thus, an absurd situation developed in which the senior officers of the JNA were insisting on upholding an illusion of 'normalcy', while all the actors on the local political stage began working on the destruction of the Federal armed forces – widely considered as the 'guardian' of the SFRJ, and surely the only armed force capable of fulfilling that task. Eventually, the senior officers of the JNA remained involved in the politics and decided to support the work of Marković's government and party. Correspondingly, it supported the establishment of the TVstation Yutel, supposed to produce balanced reports on the political developments in all of the SFRJ. Indeed, having already acquired the technology necessary to run a mobile TV station, the JNA took care to provide Yutel with support in the form of ground equipment and four SA.341H Gazelle helicopters modified to relay the TV-images. This support was referred to as Projekat Oplenac.[1]

In 1990, the HAS *Vranica* was finished, at Batajnica AB for two MiG-29 jets in the QRA. Modelled on the projects that Yugoslav companies built for Iraq, a shelter was made that was a closed unit for the accommodation of two aircraft, pilots, and technicians from the duty team, along with fuel and missiles. (Aleksandar Radić)

Croatian people to elect their leaders.[2]

The result was a rift within the senior officers. Despite Agotić's opposition, the hardliners then formed a team consisting of officers at the HQ of V Corps, tasked with establishing collaborative networks within the AoR of this corps – so also within areas not covered by its units' official tasks. The official purpose was to monitor the 'potential vulnerability of the armed forces': actually, and for all practical purposes, this 'special team' was spying not only on Agotić, but all other officers assigned to V Corps RV i PVO, as well as local political leaders in Croatia and Bosnia and Herzegovina.

Meanwhile, in reaction to the growing internal security challenge, in late 1989 the General Staff of the JNA devised Plan Radan for the case of massive public disorder or even an armed rebellion. This was not particularly detailed and left it to local commanders to develop their own planning according to the specifics of their areas of responsibility: the JNA was only to provide reinforcements as necessary. However, at least on paper, Plan Radan enabled the quick concentration of powerful units, all theoretically subordinated to the same commander. In reality it dictated the establishment of two parallel command structures, each with its own chain of command. In attempt to solve this contradiction, a meeting of top air force commanders was held in early 1990 at the Command of the RV i PVO in Zemun (a western suburb of Belgrade). During this meeting, Colonel Slobodan Rakočević – a representative of what was known as the 'hard-line pro-Yugoslavs' – demanded that the air force develop its own plan for covert action, Plan Proboj. This envisaged an intensive collection of intelligence on the work of political leaders in constituent republics, the local structures responsible for public security, and diverse civilian services. The Chief of Security of V Corps RV i PVO, Colonel Imra Agotić, openly opposed such a plan, and explained to his colleagues that it was the legal right of the

JRV i PVO in 1990

As of 1990, the basic flying unit of the air force was a squadron ('eskadrila') of 12-16 aircraft. Two, sometimes three squadrons were controlled by a brigade or a regiment: brigades controlled units equipped with different types of aircraft, while regiments controlled squadrons equipped with the same type of aircraft. The sole exception to this rule was the VVA – the Air Force Academy: this was organised into regiments with mixed equipment.

At the operational level, in late 1990 I Corps RV i PVO was still the most-important and best-equipped of its three operational-level units. Its most important air defence unit was 204th Fighter Aviation Regiment: based at Batajnica, this controlled two squadrons, of which one was equipped with MiG-29 and the other with MiG-21 interceptors. The second most-important combat unit of I Corps was 97th Aviation Brigade, which controlled two squadrons equipped with Jastreb and Galeb-4 light strikers, a squadron of J-22 Orao reconnaissance fighters, an anti-submarine squadron with a mixed fleet operating Soviet-made Kamov Ka-25PL and Ka-28s, as well as Mil Mi-14PL helicopters, and a squadron equipped with Mil Mi-8 transport and assault helicopters.

The structure of III and V Corps RV i PVO was similar in so far as each had:

- one fighter aviation regiment including two squadrons of MiG-21 interceptors
- one aviation brigade (98th and 82nd, respectively) with one reconnaissance squadron and two fighter-bomber-squadrons
- one brigade operating a mix of transport aircraft and transport and assault helicopters

Table 3: MiG-21s and MiG-29s of the JRV i PVO, October 1990

Type	Number of Aircraft	Notes
MiG-29	14	
MiG-29UB	2	
MiG-21bis	77	available in two variants: L-17 with navigational system Polyot-01, and L-17K with the ARL-SM
MiG-21M	14	mostly powered by the R-13-300 engine and thus equal to the MiG-21MF
MiG-21MF	4	equipped with US-made LORAP reconnaissance pods including the KA-112A camera
MiG-21PFM	16	
MiG-21R	10	
MiG-21UM	18	
MiG-21US	5	
MiG-21U-400/600	6	

Important support for the RV i PVO was provided through efficient overhaul in domestic plants. The Zmaj Works in Velika Gorica carried out overhauls on the MiG-21bis after 850 hours Time Between Overhaul or 10 years, whichever limit expired first. In July 1989 the aircraft from the photograph, serial 17171, was admitted for medium overhaul and in August 1990, after works, was returned to 117th FAR in which it flew during the civil war in 1991 and 1992. (plant Zmaj)

The RV i PVO had one squadron of MiG-21 reconnaissance aircraft. The standard aerial reconnaissance pod for a MiG-21R was the D with seven cameras for daytime photography, which was located on the central pylon of aircraft serial 26103. In November 1990, it flew over from Bihać AB to Pleso AB, for a general overhaul at the Zmaj plant and works lasted until the beginning of the civil war. 26103 was one of four aircraft that moved during the relocation of the plant to Serbia in December 1991. (Krila armije)

The balance of the RV i PVO – one mixed aviation brigade (including heavier transport aircraft, VIP-transports, aircraft for ELINT purposes and aerial survey), and one fire-fighting squadron – were subordinated directly to the High Command of the air force.[3]

Furthermore, the High Command of the RV i PVO was in control of the Air Force Academy. The VVA was organised into three regiments, one responsible for screening, one for basic training, and one for training of flight instructors. Its units were equipped with Utva-75 piston-engine trainers, G-2 and G-4 jet trainers, and with J-22 Oraos, Gazelles and Mi-8s.

Overall, as of 31 October 1990, the RV i PVO had a total of 860 aircraft and helicopters (including examples undergoing overhauls or repairs) – which by June 1991 were organised as listed in Table 4. Notably, there was no army aviation as a separate structure within the JNA and the RV i PVO, instead, each of the MDs was assigned a squadron of Gazelle helicopters. Administratively, these were kept within the control of the air force.

MiGs of Yugoslavia

From the early 1960s, the fighter element of the JRV i PVO was dominated by Soviet-made MiG-21s. After starting with the MiG-21F-13, through the following two decades, the air force continued acquiring additional variants in the form of the MiG-21PFM, MiG-21M, MiG-21MF, and MiG-21bis – in addition to two-seat conversion trainers (with combat capability), like the MiG-21U-400, MiG-21U-600, MiG-21US, and MiG-21UM. Under Plan Jedinstvo's concept of territorial defence, all of these were concentrated into three regiments, with a total of six squadrons. In the event of an emergency, these units would be reinforced by one reconnaissance squadron home-based at Bihać AB, and another fighter squadron home-based at Pula, which in peacetime served as advanced training assets for pilots fresh from the VVA. A modernisation of fighter aviation regiments was initiated only in 1987, when a total 16 much more advanced MiG-29s were acquired from the USSR: they replaced MiG-21s in just a single squadron of one of three regiments.

The main MiG-21 base in Yugoslavia of the late 1980s – and, indeed, the most advanced air base of the entire JRV i PVO – was

Due to the war, the ambition of the RV i PVO to introduce a new domestic fighter in the mid-1990s, for which models were made but no name was chosen, was not to be realised. (Zdenko Molnar)

Bihać AB. This included the underground Objekt Klek, constructed into the 3,500-metre-high Plješevica Mountain on the border between Croatia and Bosnia and Herzegovina, which could accommodate up to 60 MiG-21s of the three squadrons home-based there.[4] Bihać AB was constructed with a built-in capability to survive a direct nuclear strike and operate autonomously for up to 30 days. As of the late 1980s, there was a plan to replace MiG-21s of one of the locally-based squadrons with MiG-29, and the work on the related modification to some entrances into Objekt Klek was started, but did not advance very far before the war began. The second major MiG-21 base, Slatina AB outside Priština, had a simpler underground element: Objekt Rudnik. This was much smaller than Objekt Klek but was also designed to protect and operate MiG-21 aircraft. The same was true for underground facilities at Divulje AB, outside the port of Split and the adjacent main port of Lora, the main base of the Yugoslav Navy.

However, the central – and the largest – air base of the RV i PVO was Batajnica, west of Belgrade. Located on a plain next to the River Danube, this offered no opportunities for underground construction, but a number of standard-sized concrete aircraft shelters, covered by a thick layer of earth, were constructed there as on most other air bases in the SFRJ, starting in the 1950s. Moreover, in 1990, a hardened aircraft shelter (HAS) *Vranica* was constructed at Batajnica AB, designed to protect two MiG-29s held on the quick reaction alert (QRA).

The primary role of the Yugoslav MiG-21 and MiG-29 units was air defence. However, because the mass of the RV i PVO's fleet of fighter-bombers consisted of light aircraft with relatively limited payload capacity, both types had an important secondary role of ground attack, including close air support (CAS). For this purpose, during the 1980s British-made Hunting BL.755 cluster bomb units (CBUs), and domestic PLAB-350J incendiary bombs were adapted to the MiG-21s. Moreover, MiG-29s arrived together with a large complement of Soviet-made BetAB-500 concrete-piercing bombs, KMGU CBUs, and 80mm S-8KO unguided rockets. Finally, both types could be armed with Soviet-made S-5K 57mm and S-24B 240mm unguided rockets, and a wide range of imported and domestically manufactured bombs of 100, 250, and 500kg. Yugoslav MiG-21 and MiG-29 pilots underwent regular and intensive training: indeed, during the 1980s, the JRV i PVO was renowned for flying more training sorties annually than the Israeli air force. The total fighter complement of the air force as of autumn 1990 was as listed in Tables 3 and 4. Notably, as of 31 October, 11 MiG-21s (including nine MiG-21bis, one MiG-21US and one MiG-21U) were undergoing overhauls, and thus not available for service with their units.

Novi Avion

Before the war, the RV i PVO had expected, with great hope, a decision to be made by the Federal authorities on the initiation of a project for the development of a domestic supersonic multirole fighter-bomber, colloquially known as the New Aircraft ('Novi Avion', NA, code-named *Sloboda*, or 'freedom'). The presidency of the SFRJ had accepted a related proposal in November 1984, and a decision was taken to pursue its further development with technological support from developed countries – also in order to share resulting costs. However, no suitable partner was ever found, and the decision was taken to continue with the project independently. The next step was to let the VTI develop a conceptual design with help from Avions Marcel Dassault-Breguet Aviation (AMD-BA) in France, and British Aerospace (BAe, nowadays BAE Systems) in Great Britain. Progress was slow, nevertheless, and prompted the acquisition of MiG-29s to cover the gap until the NA would become available during the second half of the 1990s. Ultimately, the RV i PVO planned to acquire about 150 of the new fighters, which were to replace about 60 early MiG-21s, which were due to reach the end of their useful lives in 1994-1998.

Although the requirement was thus clearly defined, and the VTI and various other institutes and commercial enterprises were working on research and development of different related systems, assemblies and sub-assemblies, the NA was never formally launched before the outbreak of the war.

Attack Aviation

In the terminology of the RV i PVO the category of 'fighter-bomber' aircraft stipulated trans-sonic and sub-sonic aircraft of indigenous design (usually designed by the VTI), manufactured by the Soko Works in Mostar and Utva in Pančevo with the support of technological partners from the West, and powered by Rolls-Royce engines. The first generation of Yugoslav jet-powered light strikers was the two-seat trainer from the G-2 Galeb series. First flown in 1961, these were powered with Rolls-Royce Viper Mk 22-6 engines, with 11.12 kN thrust. The single-seat derivative of the Galeb was the Jastreb, first flown in 1965 and powered by the slightly stronger Viper Mk.531, with 13.32 kN thrust. The avionics and armament of both jets were to the same standard, with only minor differences: the nose of the Galeb housed two 12.7mm Colt-Browning M3 machine guns, that of the Jastreb housed three. The Galeb could carry two bombs of up to 100kg and two launch-rails for US-made 5-inch HVAR unguided rockets under its wings; the Jastreb could take two bombs up to 250kg and launch-rails for six HVARs.

In 1966, the RV i PVO introduced to service the next generation of training jets. Originally designated N-60 (Factory designation 'Galeb-2') this variant entered service with the VVA at Zemunik serving for basic jet training and could also carry weapons. Moreover, the instructor pilots flying them received regular tactical training and in the case of emergency they could reinforce attack units.

In 1969, the RV i PVO introduced to service the next variant of the Jastreb, which received the internal designation J-21. Four years later, the reconnaissance version – suitably designated the IJ-21 – followed. Finally, in 1975 the NJ-21 Jastreb entered service. Both the J-21 and the NJ-21 differed from the original Galeb in being based on the fuselage of the original Jastreb, and by being powered by the stronger Viper Mk. 531. Ultimately, they replaced the remaining F-84Gs and RF-84Gs, as well as T-33A/TV-2s.

Certainly enough, the combat value of the Jastreb was modest in comparison to the veteran Korean-war jets it replaced: it carried around half of tonne of combat load and had three, instead of six machine guns. However, their key positive characteristics – at least according to the assessments of the RV i PVO – was that it could be operated under primitive conditions, including from grass runways, and required only a bare minimum of maintenance over extended periods of time. That was not a fact that would realistically tip the scales during a war and therefore from the late 1960s work commenced on the Orao – a new attack and reconnaissance aircraft with two engines. From 1970 the project was run on a 50:50 share basis with the Romanian aviation industry. In 1974 one prototype took off in each country. After solving difficulties with the poor thrust-to-weight ratio, it was introduced to service in Yugoslavia in 1981, in the form of a reconnaissance variant, the IJ-22, and the trainer INJ-22, powered by two Viper Mk.632-41 engines with 17.80kN of thrust each. In the meantime, new production technology was introduced with the support of Dassault and from 1985 J-22 attack aircraft and two-seater NJ-22s arrived with units. The initial series of single-seaters had a basic engine like the IJ/INJ-22, but during production, there was a switch to Mk.633-41 engines with 22.40kN thrust in afterburner – which was manufactured by the Orao Works in Rajlovac (a suburb of Sarajevo), and subsequently installed in all the NJ-22s. Oraos were armed with a 23mm GSh-23LY twin-barrelled gun installed low in the fuselage and had four underwing hardpoints rated at 500kg each. The latter could carry pods for 57mm and 128mm unguided rockets and such imported ordnance as US-made Hughes AGM-65B Mavericks, British Hunting BL.755 CBUs, and French-made Durandal runway-cratering bombs.

A pair of J-22 Orao aircraft, from the 238th Squadron, armed with British-made BL-755 cluster bombs, in flight above the Slovenian mountains. (Mladen Savić)

A J-21 Jastreb light attack aircraft with three 12.7mm machine guns and a maximum of two 250kg bombs and four 5-inch HVAR rockets (weighing 764kg) represented half of the combat power of a F-84G Thunderjet aircraft, which had left a deep mark in the history of the RV i PVO from 1953 to 1974. When Jastreb aircraft replaced the F-84G, it was estimated that the domestic aircraft had a large advantage because it is able to take off and land from a grass field or a partially damaged runway. In practice during the civil war, this was never utilised. (Aleksandar Radić)

In 1991, three training squadrons of the VVA had Galeb-4s. Besides being trained as instructors, pilots from this unit had full combat training in order to increase the number of combat aircraft available during war. (Davor Lukić)

A result of a complete re-design of the original G-2, but developed with economy of production in mind, was the G-4 trainer, powered by the Viper Mk.632-46 engine with 17.80kN thrust. This type received the N-62 pod including the GSh-23LY gun and four underwing hardpoints to carry bombs, including the BL.755, and unguided rockets, and quickly became not only the advanced trainer but also the standard attack aircraft of the RV i PVO.

By the time the war of 1991 erupted, there were a total of six operational fighter-bomber squadrons: two with Oraos, three with Jastrebs, and one with a mix of G-2s, G-4s, and J-21s. Three reconnaissance squadrons were equipped with IJ-22s, IJ-21s, and a mix of both, respectively, while the VVA included six squadrons, with one flying G-2s for basic training, three G-4s for advanced training, and one Oraos for attack training.

As of 31 October 1990 (at the time the Soko Works were still delivering new J-22s and G-4s), the RV i PVO was operating a total of 348 jets of domestic origin (of which 307 were operational and 41 undergoing overhauls). This inventory included 87 Oraos (45 J-22s, 14 NJ-22s, 22 IJ-22s and 6 INJ-22s), 75 G-4s, 107 Jastrebs and 79 Galeb-2s. At the time, it expected to withdraw from service all of the latter during the early 1990s and extend the production of the Orao until 1997-1998. Moreover, the VTI was working on a comprehensive upgrade of the Orao, including a new head-up display (HUD), a head-down display (HDD), and a forward-looking infra-red (FLIR) pod with a laser designator for guided bombs and AGM-65D/E Mavericks. Finally, a modification of the IJ-22 including an ELINT-pod had been in planning. Similarly, in 1986, work was launched on an upgrade of the G-4 with an electronic HUD, Soviet-made R-60 air-to-air missiles (ASCC/NATO-codename 'AA-8 Aphid'), and AGM-65 Maverick missiles.[5]

Two Learjet 25B aircraft for VIP transport had markings of the RV i PVO and they were used for the needs of the Federal Secretary for National Defence and the highest ranked generals. (Zdenko Molnar)

The small firefighting squadron with four CL-215s had a lot of work during the summer season. During the last pre-war season in 1990, they had 120 interventions and dropped 3,600 water bombs. At that time, a special law had been in preparation for the financing of the procurement of four aircraft with turboprop engines in 1993 to 1995. (Vlatko Svilar)

An-26 aircraft were used every day for the transport of passengers, freight, confidential and other mail between airports. Aircraft from 679th TAS had a dark grey nose, while 677th TAS were recognizable by their light blue nose, as with serial 71352 that was photographed in June 1990 at Batajnica airport. (Zdenko Molnar)

Transport Aviation

In the category of auxiliary aviation, as of 31 October 1990 the RV i PVO had 34 different aircraft. The largest part of the fleet consisted of 15 twin-engined Antonov An-26Bs which were divided between two squadrons. The only four-engined aircraft was a single Antonov An-12B, acquired in 1971: it was last flown on 21 November 1990 and thus never saw action during the war. As a replacement, the air force planned to acquire two new Lockheed L-100-30 Hercules, but this idea was never realised. A single Dassault Falcon 50 and two Learjet 25Bs were used as VIP-transports, together with six Yak-40s. One of the latter was modified as an ELINT-gathering aircraft and used for the calibration of ground radio-navigation devices in a separate Federal Direction for Traffic Control Flight. Five Polish-made Antonov An-2TD aircraft were used for the training of paratroopers, while two Do.28D2 were deployed for aero-photogrammetric recordings on behalf of the Military-geographic institute. Finally, four Canadair CL.215 fire-fighting aircraft were operated from the Zemunik AB (though funded from a civilian budget) for fire-fighting purposes along the Adriatic Coast.

Helicopters

During the time before the civil war the helicopter fleet of the RV i PVO was undergoing major expansion. The SA.342L Gazelle was in serial production at the Soko Works in Mostar, and procurement and licence-production of new medium-class helicopter aircraft was planned as a replacement for the elderly Mi-8 helicopters.

As of 31 October 1990, the RV i PVO had 242 rotor-wing aircraft – 221 in units and 21 undergoing overhauls. Of these, 81 were Mi-8s, which were deployed for transport and assault purposes. However, the fleet of 150 SA.341H and SA.342L Gazelles was much larger: of these, 41 SA.341Hs and 20 SA.342Ls were utilised for training at the VVA, for liaison, and in various auxiliary units of the RV i PVO, ground, and naval forces. Attack squadrons operated a total of 33 SA.341Hs with French-made APX M334.02 sights, and 33 SA.42L with M334.40 sights: both sub-variants could be armed with up to four Soviet-made 9M14 Malyutka (ASCC/NATO-codename 'AT-3 Sagger') anti-tank guided missiles (ATGMs), and two 9M32 Strela-2M infra-red homing air-to-air missiles. Both became colloquially known as 'Gama' – which was an acronym for 'Gazelle-Malyutka'.[6]

For reconnaissance and correction of artillery fire on behalf of the land forces 18 specially modified SA.341Hs (locally designated the Hi-42 Hera) were in service with the RV i PVO. The Heras (which stood for 'helicopter-radio') were equipped with an M334.25 targeting sight including a laser rangefinder, a device for radiological reconnaissance, an advanced navigation system and the UGAR-3S radio.

The RV i PVO also had two Gazelles modified to the Hs-42 standard, equipped with a rescue winch and used for search and rescue (SAR) purposes, and two Alouette III helicopters operated for liaison purposes on behalf of the 1st MD. The sole anti-submarine squadron was equipped with four Ka-25PLs, two Ka-28s, and three Mi-14PL anti-submarine helicopters: two further Ka-25Pls were undergoing overhauls at the 770th Plant Kacha, in the Crimea in the USSR, and never returned. In addition to their original armament of Soviet origin, Ka-25PLs and Mi-14PLs were equipped with US-made Mk.44 322.6mm guided torpedoes. Since December 1987, they and the Ka-28s were also armed with advanced APR-2E Jastreb-E guided torpedoes, which could reach a maximum depth of 600m, but due to their high price only eight such weapons were acquired.

Piston-Engined Aircraft

Two indigenous Utva-66 fixed-wing liaison aircraft were assigned to the headquarters of every brigade, regiment and squadron of the RV i PVO: as of October 1990 there were 44 of them were in the inventory. Furthermore, the air force operated a total of 25 Utva-75 basic trainers used for the screening course before admission of cadets to the VVA. The plan to replace the Utva-75s with new, much more powerful and advanced Lasta trainers was well-developed, but only one prototype was undergoing testing as of the early 1990s.

Competition for Weapons of the Slovenian TO

Starting in 1990, almost all the leaderships of the constituent republics of the SFRJ initiated clandestine activities in the forming of ethnicity-based armed forces. Initially, this process was run using legal mechanisms, usually by the local ministry of interior, or the TO. The SSNO was quick in recognizing that the well-stockpiled warehouses of the TO were likely to become the primary source of arms for such formations. For example, as of 31 December 1990, the warehouses of the Slovenian TO contained the following air-defence armament:

A Kamov K-25PL during a landing approach to its home base of Divulje, which was built on the site of a water aerodrome from the period between the two World Wars. The photograph originates from 1990 at a time when the political atmosphere in Dalmatia was very hot. (Aleksandar Kelić, Media Center Odbrana)

- 279 20mm single-barrel guns
- 24 20mm M55 triple-barrel guns
- 205 Zastava M75
- 59 M38s (Yugoslav designation for the famous German Flak 38)
- 10 Oerlikons
- 44 Bofors M1 and M12s
- 99 Strela-2M grip stocks

Correspondingly, on 14 May 1990, the SSNO issued an order for all TO armament to be placed under the control of the JNA: from that point onward, a significant portion of the armament in question was transferred to the JNA's storage depots, but a significant quantity had already been removed from the warehouses of the Slovenian

Table 4: RV i PVO, Order of Battle, June 1991		
COMMAND OF AF&AD, Zemun		
138th TRANSPORT AVIATION BRIGADE, HQ Batajnica		
675th Transport Aviation Squadron	Batajnica	4 Yak-40, 1 Falcon 50, 2 Learjet 25B
678th Mixed Aviation Squadron	Batajnica	2 Do-28D2, 2 HT-40
890th Mixed Helicopter Squadron	Batajnica	6 HT-40, 3 HO-45, 1 HO-42, 1 Hi-42
63rd Parachute Brigade, Niš		
VTI, Beograd		
Air Test Centre, Batajnica		
Flight Test Squadron	Batajnica	2 L-17, 5 J-22, 1 NJ-22, 1 IJ-22, 4 N-62, 1 HT-40, 1 HN-45M, 1 HO-45, 1 N-63, 2 V-53, 1 V-51
Aeronautical Medical Institute, Batajnica		
975th Aviation Training Centre, Sombor		
672nd Automotive Training Centre, Kovin		
160th Air-Technical base, Pančevo		
676th Firefighting Aviation Squadron	Zemunik	3 CL-215, 1 HO-45, 1 HO-42
321st Signal Battalion, Nedžarići		
322nd Signal Battalion, Novi Sad		
333rd Engineer Battalion, Pančevo		
170th Intelligence Center, Zemun		
Counterintelligence Group, Zemun		
I Detachment, Skoplje		
II Detachment, Zagreb		
III Detachment, Sarajevo		
99th Military Police Company, Zemun (had a platoon with 3 TAB-71 armoured personnel carriers)		
I Corps JRV i PVO, HQ Beograd		
Liaison Aviation Squadron	Batajnica	2 HT-40, 2 Alouette III, 2 HO-45, 1 V-51
97th Aviation Brigade, HQ Mostar		
240th Fighter-Bomber Aviation Squadron	Mostar	14 J-21, 1 IJ-21, 3 NJ-21, 4 N-60, 2 V-51
252nd Fighter-Bomber Aviation Squadron	Batajnica	4 N-62, 2 N-62T, 10 J-21, 6 N-60, 1 V-51
352nd Reconnaissance Aviation Squadron	Mostar	9 IJ-22, 3 INJ-22, 1 INJ-22M
784th Anti-submarine Helicopter Squadron	Divulje	2 HP-46, 3 HP-44, 4 HP-43, 4 HT-40
790th Transport Helicopter Squadron	Divulje	10 HT-40
204th Fighter Aviation Regiment, HQ Batajnica		
126th Fighter Aviation Squadron	Batajnica	15 L-17, 2 NL-16, 1 NL-12, 2 V-51
127th Fighter Aviation Squadron	Batajnica	14 L-18, 2 NL-18, 1 V-51
250th Air Defence Rocket Brigade, HQ Batajnica		
1st Rocket Battalion, Mladenovac		
2nd Rocket Battalion, Smederevo		
3rd Rocket Battalion, Batajnica		
4th Rocket Battalion, Pančevo		
5th Rocket Battalion, Jakovo		
6th Rocket Battalion, Zuce		
1st Rocket Technical Battalion, Sremčica		

Table 4: RV i PVO, Order of Battle, June 1991 *(continued)*		
2nd Rocket Technical Battalion, Zuce		
1st Aerial Surveillance Regiment, HQ Banjica		
20th Air Surveillance Battalion, Stari Banovci		
61st Air Surveillance Battalion, Split		
130th Air Base, HQ Rajlovac		
171st Air Base, HQ Mostar – Ortiješ and Jasenica		
177th Air Base, HQ Batajnica		
399th Air Base, HQ Tuzla		
500th Air Base, HQ Divulje		
210th Signal Battalion, HQ Banjica, Beograd		
III Corps JRV i PVO, HQ Niš		
98th Aviation Brigade, HQ Petrovac		
241st Fighter-Bomber Aviation Squadron	Petrovac	14 J-22, 2 NJ-22, 2 V-51
247th Fighter-Bomber Aviation Squadron	Petrovac	19 J-21, 1 NJ-21, 3 N-60, 1 V-51
354th Reconnaissance Aviation Squadron	Ladevci	17 IJ-21, 3 N-60, 2 V-51
119th Aviation Brigade, HQ Niš		
2 V-51		
677th Transport Aviation Squadron	Niš	6 T-70, 2 An-2TD
787th Transport Helicopter Squadron	Niš	15 HT-40
712th Anti-Armor Helicopter Squadron	Niš	17 HN-45M, 1 HO-45
714th Anti-Armor Helicopter Squadron	Ladevci	16 HN-42M, 1 HO-42
83rd Fighter Aviation Regiment, HQ Priština		
123rd Fighter Aviation Squadron	Priština	16 L-17, 1 NL-16, 1 NL-14, 2 NL-12, 2 V-51
130th Fighter Aviation Squadron	Priština	13 L-15, 2 L-17, 1 NL-16, 1 NL-14, 1 NL-12, 2 V-51
450th Air Defence Rocket Regiment, HQ Petrovac		
1st Rocket Battalion, Skoplje		
2nd Rocket Battalion, Petrovac		
3rd Rocket Battalion, Ćojlije		
4th Rocket Battalion, Skoplje		
1st Rocket Technical Battalion, Ćojlije		
3rd AIR SURVEILLANCE REGIMENT, HQ Niš		
31st Air Surveillance Battalion, Kraljevo		
58th Air Surveillance Battalion, Titograd		
161st Air Base, HQ Niš		
165th Air Base, HQ Petrovac		
285th Air Base, HQ Ladevci		
423rd Air Base, HQ Titograd		Maintenance of 7 J-20 and 1 V-51 for TO
492nd Air Base, HQ Priština		
112th Signal Battalion, Niš		
359th Engineer Battalion, Ladevci		
3rd Electronic Intelligence Center, Niš		
V Corps JRV i PVO, HQ Zagreb		
82nd Aviation Brigade, HQ Cerklje		
237th Fighter-Bomber Aviation Squadron	Cerklje	17 J-21, 2 NJ-21, 5 N-60, 1 V-51

Table 4: RV i PVO, Order of Battle, June 1991 *(continued)*		
238th Fighter-Bomber Aviation Squadron	Cerklje	11 J-22, 1 NJ-22, 1 V-51
351st Reconnaissance Aviation Squadron	Cerklje	4 IJ-22, 1 NJ-22, 1 INJ-22, 8 IJ-21, 2 N-60
111th Aviation Brigade, HQ Pleso		
679th Transport Aviation Squadron	Pleso	7 T-70, 1 An-2TD, 2 V-51
780th Transport Helicopter Squadron		17 HT-40
711th Anti-Armor Helicopter Squadron	Lučko	16 HN-42M, 1 HO-42
713th Anti-Armor Helicopter Squadron	Lučko	4 HN-45M, 1 HO-45
117th Fighter Aviation Regiment, HQ Bihać		
124th Fighter Aviation Squadron	Bihać	16 L-17, 3 NL-16, 1 NL-14
125th Fighter Aviation Squadron	Bihać	16 L-17, 2 NL-16, 2 NL-12, 1 V-51
352nd Reconnaissance Aviation Squadron	Bihać	4 L-15M, 8 L-14i, 3 L-14, 1 NL-14, 1 V-51
155th Air Defence Rocket Regiment, HQ Kerestinec		
1st Rocket Battalion, Cerklje		
2nd Rocket Battalion, Karlovac		
3rd Rocket Battalion, Sisak		
4th Rocket Battalion, Zabok		
1st Rocket Technical Battalion		
350th Air Defence Rocket Regiment, HQ Vrhnika		
1st Rocket Battalion, Šentvid		
2nd Rocket Battalion, Ljubljana Polje		
3rd Rocket Battalion, Logatec		
4th Rocket Battalion, Postojna		
1st Rocket Technical Battalion, Vrhnika		
5th Aerial Surveillance Regiment, HQ Pleso		
51st Air Surveillance Battalion, Željava		
91st Air Surveillance Battalion, Vrhnika		
84th Air Base, HQ Zemunik		
151st Air Base, HQ Pleso		
200th Air Base, HQ Bihać		
258th Air Base, HQ Pula		
474th Air Base, HQ Cerklje		
289th Signal Battalion, Lučko		
379th Engineer Battalion, Zagreb		
344th Engineer Company		
5th Electronic Intelligence Centre, Velika Buna		
Air Force Academy, HQ Zemunik		
105th FIGHTER-BOMBER AVIATION REGIMENT, HQ Zemunik		
249th Fighter-Bomber Aviation Squadron	Zemunik	14 N-62, 10 V-53, 1 V-51
251st Fighter-Bomber Aviation Squadron	Zemunik	31 N-60 (23 in flight order and 8 without resources), 10 V-53, 1 V-51
333rd Mixed Aviation Squadron	Zemunik	7 N-62 (aerobatic team), 20 N-60, 1 An-2TD, 1 HO-45N
172nd Fighter-Bomber Aviation Regiment, HQ Titograd		
239th Fighter-Bomber Aviation Squadron	Titograd	18 N-62
242nd Fighter-Bomber Aviation Squadron	Titograd	10 J-22, 11 NJ-22, 3 NJ-21, 2 V-51, 1 HO-45
185th Fighter-Bomber Aviation Regiment, HQ Pula		
129th Fighter Aviation Squadron	Pula	12 L-14, 7 NL-16, 1 V-51

Table 4: RV i PVO, Order of Battle, June 1991 *(continued)*		
229th Fighter-Bomber Aviation Squadron	Pula	17 N-62, 1 V-51, 1 HO-45
107th Mixed Aviation Regiment (Training), HQ Mostar-Jesenice		
782nd Helicopter Squadron (Training)	Mostar-Jesenice	10 HT-40, 17 HN-45M, 14 HO-42, 2 Hsn-42
Air Force Gymnasium 'Marsal Tito'		

Deputy Chief-of-Staff Armed Forces for Air Force and Air Defence, Belgrade	
Air Department	
Air-Technical Department	
Air Defence Department	
Air Surveillance Department	
Centre of higher military schools of RV i PVO, Beograd	
Air Force and Air Defence Education Centre, Rajlovac	
Air Defence Education Centre, Zadar	
Air Force Technical Military Academy, Žarkovo-Beograd	
Zmaj Works, Velika Gorica	9 L-17, 1 L-14, 2 L-14i, 2 NL-16, 1 NL-14, 8 N-62/N-62T, 3 J-21, 1 NJ-21, 12 N-60 and Iraqi aircraft – 10 MiG-23ML and 8 MiG-21bis ('SMT')
Moma Stanojlović Works, Batajnica	1 J-22, 8 IJ-22, 1 INJ-22, 2 J-21, 3 IJ-21, 2 NJ-21, 2 T-70, 1 CL-215, 1 An-2TD, 8 V-51, 2 V-53 from RV i PVO and 13 from VSJ, 10 HT-40 on overhaul and 4 on modifications to ELINT version, 1 HN-42M, 12 HO/Hsn-42. 4 Zlin 526 from VSJ and 4 Mi-2 in preparation for sale to private users
Kosmos Works, Banja Luka	
Orao Works, Rajlovac	

Table 5: Flying Units directly subordinated to Military Districts		
891st Reconnaissance and Liaison Aviation Squadron	Petrovac 1st Flight Petrovac 2nd Flight Niš 3rd Flight Golubovci	3 HO-45, 7 HI-42, 4 HO-42
894th Reconnaissance and Liaison Aviation Squadron	Pleso 1st Flight Pleso 2nd Flight Brnik	2 HO-45, 3 Hi-42, 5 HO-42
895th Reconnaissance and Liaison Aviation Squadron	Divulje	1 HO-45, 2 HI-42, 1 HO-42
896th Reconnaissance and Liaison Aviation Squadron	Batajnica 1st Flight Batajnica 2nd Flight Rajlovac	2 HO-45, 5 HI-42, 3 HO-42

TO in particular, and its whereabouts became a matter of a major dispute between Belgrade and Ljubljana. Certainly enough, on 15 May 1990, the HQ of the Slovenian TO issued an order for its units to hand over all of their armament to the JNA's depots by midnight of 19 May. However, the commander of the Slovenian TO, Lieutenant-General Ivan Hočevar (a pilot by profession), stuck to the order from the SSNO. However, during the following days, and in a rapid sequence of events, the first multi-party government of Slovenia came into being and was officially inaugurated on 16 May 1990. Three days later, this government suspended most of the decisions of the last single-party government, including the hand-over of the TO's armament. Thus, the JNA found itself in control of slightly more than 70 percent of the armament of the Slovenian TO, while the rest became the core with which the Slovenes subsequently formed a parallel structure, loyal only to the authorities in Ljubljana. This new structure was officially formalised on 4 October 1990, when Ljubljana officially established the Territorial Defence of Slovenia (TOS).[7]

Moreover, during the second half of 1990, and in great secrecy, the government of Slovenia established the Manoeuvre Structures of National Protection (Manevarske strukture narodne zaščite – MSNZ). Controlled by the ministry of interior in Ljubljana, this body represented the core of a subsequently established parallel paramilitary structure loyal solely to the Slovenian authorities.[8] Around the same time, Slovenia clandestinely ran Operation Bor, an effort to acquire additional armament from abroad, foremost including Armbrust anti-tank rocket launchers and 5.56mm SAR-80 assault rifles, both of Western origin.

Finally, the government of Slovenia took over all the procedures related to recruiting for the regular military service and the organisation of the TO. On 29 March 1991 it unilaterally subordinated the Slovenian TO to its control and severed all links to the Federal

Ground-based Air Defences

The Yugoslav air defences were centred on an enormous quantity of light anti-aircraft artillery pieces: no fewer than 9,344 guns of various types, ranging in calibre from 20mm to 57mm were available as of October 1990. The most numerous of these were the famous 20mm Crvena Zastava M75 single-barrel and M55 three-barrel cannons based on a local derivative of the Hispano HS.404 gun. Out of a total of 7,135 such pieces, 240 M55s were installed on the lightly armoured, self-propelled 4WD vehicles designated BOV-3; 3,554 were towed (including 84 of the basic version, 83 of the M55A2, and 2,203 hydraulically-driven M55A3s), 1,048 M55A4 (with the J171 fire-control system), and 136 Mk.IIs (essentially cannons taken from disused Mosquito fighter-bombers installed on the chassis of the famous German Flak 38, with the sight from the M55 cannon). The JNA also operated 700 (out of 789 originally acquired) Czechoslovak-manufactured 30mm M53/59 and M53/70 self-propelled guns, and 110 Soviet-made ZSU-57-2 self-propelled-guns and 57/2 towed anti-aircraft guns. While all of these weapons were relatively obsolete, nothing similar could be said about 114 Bofors L/70 40mm anti-aircraft guns which were acquired together with Giraffe 40 radars and laser-rangefinders. The bulk of anti-aircraft artillery was deployed for the defence of RV i PVO air bases.

The TO units were equipped with 2,762 single-barrel M75 and some Flak 38s, but also a large number of obsolete, or at least vintage, guns from the Second World War, including 143 Soviet-made 25mm M40s, 339 37mm M39s, and 573 40mm Bofors L/60s in both the US-made- M1 and the British-made M12 variants. Air defence batteries destined for the defence of major factories were allocated a total of 219 four-barrel, 120 twin-barrel and 240 single-barrel guns of various calibres, and 380 12.7mm Browning M2HB machine guns.

During the 1970s and the 1980s, the JNA and the RV i PVO accumulated a huge number of MANPADS. Domestic production turned out as many as 4,400 grip stocks for Strela-2Ms, and these were in widespread service with both the JNA and the TO. There was a project for the development and production of a modern 40mm anti-aircraft gun – in a self-propelled and towed variant – but this was never realised because of the war.

When it comes to heavier SAMs, the JNA had six regiments equipped with a total of 120 'transporter, erector, launchers' (TELs) for 2K12 Kub-M, while the RV i PVO operated a total of 49 trailer-mobile launchers for Neva-M and 25 trailer-mobile launchers for Dvina and Volkhov SAM-systems. Finally, the JNA had 126 9K31 Strela-1M self-propelled launchers in service. The newest system of this kind was eight launchers of 9K35 Strela-10 (ASCC/NATO-codename 'SA-13 Gopher') surface-to-air missiles and as of 1989-1990 Yugoslavia was in the process of acquiring the licence for their domestic production, with the intention of installing them on the chassis of the indigenous M-80A infantry fighting vehicle. (*Continued opposite*)

The TO of Slovenia had a squadron with twelve J-20 Kraguj light attack aircraft. Reservists would be called up twice per year to undergo flight and combat refreshment training in the TO. (Miha Kos via Tomaž Perme)

There were three regiments in the RV i PVO that each had four battalions of SAM S-12M Neva-M, for the defence of Slovenia, Belgrade and Macedonia. Regular firings were carried out at the range on cape Kamenjak, the narrowest part of the Istrian peninsula. (Krila armije)

The armament inventory was included the specially designed M86 military police armoured combat vehicle armed with a 12.7mm machinegun and six launchers for smoke grenades. The photograph was taken in January 1991 during the training of the 9th Military Police Battalion in Knin, a unit that took a significant participation in battles during 1991 in the area of northern Dalmatia. (Zoran Milovanović, Media Center Odbrana)

The training of AAG Bofors L/70 crews in the 130th Air Defence Light Artillery and Missile Battalion from 130th Air Base in Rajlovac in 1991. (Mladen Savić)

The RV i PVO had units of military police that practiced protection of infrastructure in 1990 and 1991. The photographs show soldiers from the military police platoon of the 130th AB from Rajlovac. In wartime, a platoon mobilised reservists and formed a company, as was planned in all 15 air bases of the RV i PVO. (Mladen Savić)

authorities. Unsurprisingly, the General Staff of the JNA reacted by developing several 'war plans':

- Nabava, for a take-over of all the armament of the TO
- Jezero, for establishment of reception centres for members of the JNA expected to defect from the Slovenian TO
- Kamen, which aimed to secure all the international border crossings in Slovenia

Build-up of the Croatian Police

From 1 January 1990, and amid growing inter-ethnic tensions, the Croatian government initiated a reform of its Ministry of Internal Affairs (MUP). Instead of the highly centralised hierarchy, it introduced a highly decentralised organisation. After the first multi-party elections in Croatia, held on 30 May 1990, a new government was inaugurated, controlled by the party that won the elections – the right-wing Croatian Democratic Union (HDZ) – led by the former general of the JNA, Franjo Tuđman. Determined to effect an independence of Croatia from the SFRJ (and heavily financed for this purpose by the Croatian diaspora abroad), Tuđman and the HDZ almost immediately initiated the establishment of embryonic armed forces within the Croatian MUP. The first step in this direction was a significant quantitative increase of the Croatian police: 1,800 cadets were recruited early during the summer and, after their parade on 5 August 1990 in Zagreb admitted for a two-month training course. Additional recruits were subsequently organised into the Reserve Police – the structures of which became the source of personnel for future combat units.

Parallel to these operations, the Croatian authorities established their own Ministry of Defence, led by the retired General of the JNA, Martin Špegelj. Amongst others, one of Špegelj's first orders was to collect as many anti-aircraft weapons of the TO as possible because he had serious concerns about the offensive power of the RV i PVO and was insistent on creating strong air defence capabilities. To the dismay of the JNA, its local commanders were not particularly consistent in the application of the take-over order from 14 May 1990, and thus at least 66 M55, M75, and Bofors anti-aircraft guns 'disappeared', while the government in Zagreb placed additional orders for the production of similar weapons with companies in Sisak, Slavonski Brod, and Osijek. By December 1990, the Croats also ran a large-scale clandestine operation of acquiring weapons from abroad. Amongst those known to have reached the republic were 40 Strela-2Ms, which were unloaded from a smuggling ship anchored off the island of Krk. The Croatian attempt to acquire a batch of US-made FIM-92A Stinger MANPADS – widely perceived as the 'best' of this kind of weapon at the time – fell through, although negotiations for an acquisition of 40 grip stocks with 10 missiles each were continued.[9]

During the politically and security-wise turbulent period of 1990-1992 the Croats had only a single AB.212 (registration YU-HBM, c/n 5569, made in 1977) for all VIP transport and intervention units. The attempt on 17 August 1990 to transport members of the police from Zagreb to Knin, the centre of the Serbian uprising, was stopped by a threat from the RV i PVO's MiG-21s. (Danijel Frka)

A still from a video taken in late summer 1991 in Slavonia, but similar to the atmosphere on 17 August 1990, with one AB.212 and two AB.206s in formation. (from documentary series *War and before the war*)

Knin Incident

The inauguration of a right-wing government with nationalist ideology in Zagreb, fuelled the claims of the Serbian nationalists that Croatia was about to turn into a Neo-Nazi state, and had to be expected to seek either an extermination or at least ethnic cleansing of the Serbs. Resulting fears prompted many Serbs living in the parts of Croatia where they formed the majority of the population to take-up arms and organise their own armed militias. These not only refused to obey the decisions of the government in Zagreb, but also forced the Croatian police out of the areas under their control. The situation came to a head for the first time in late July 1990 when members of the Serbian Democratic Party (SDS) withdrew from the HDZ-dominated parliament in Zagreb and began forming their own civic bodies to administer the communities predominantly populated by the Serbs. Next, the leadership of the SDS announced a referendum on autonomy, to which, on 16 August 1990, the Croatian Police reacted by deploying reinforcements. The Serbian militias set up a number of roadblocks in order to prevent the Croatian police from entering the areas controlled by them, some of which cut off all the traffic between Zagreb and most of Dalmatia.

On the morning of 17 August 1990, a group of Croatian police officers was lined-up in the woodland of the Police Academy in Šimunska Street in Zagreb, and an officer asked for volunteers for a 'small helicopter ride to Knin' in northern Dalmatia, about 56 kilometres north of Šibenik, that in the summer of 1990 had become the stronghold of the Serbian resistance against the new Croatian authorities. The volunteers were provided with camouflage uniforms in a pattern worn by the members of the Serbian militia and then embarked three helicopters of the Croatian police: one Agusta-Bell AB.212 (registration YU-HBM), and two Bell 206 Jet Rangers (registrations YU-HBC and YU-HBZ). At 1130hrs, all three took off towards Knin.

At the time, the Yugoslav airspace was still under the control of the Federal authorities in the form of two bodies: the flight control of the RV i PVO, and the air traffic control (ATC) of the Federal civilian authorities. The Croatian police had the responsibility to report its flight to both of them. However, in an attempt to conceal the destination of their formation, the Croats registered this 'Flight 7303' as one of helicopters operated by pilots from civilian aero clubs flying fire-fighting reconnaissance, and without mentioning a single word about Knin.

At 1148hrs, the pilot of the AB.212 reported his position to the Airport Flight Control (AKL) of Bihać AB: three minutes later, AKL Bihać advised the pilot of a single MiG-21R reconnaissance fighter of the RV i PVO underway on a routine training mission, to search for three helicopters underway low over the Ogulin area. Before the MiG could reach them, at 1207hrs all three Croatian police helicopters landed in Ogulin – without informing either the military or civilian flight-control authorities. Then, and rather suddenly, at 1314hrs, the same pilot of the Croatian AB.212 contacted the AKL Bihać once again and requested permission for a flight in the direction of Zadar, with refuelling stops in Knin and Sinj. AKL Bihać granted approval, and the helicopters took off. However, by 1316hrs, the information about this movement had reached the Chief of the Combat Command

Centre of V Corps RV i PVO, who informed his superiors. The latter reacted with an order for the helicopters to land immediately, and thus at 1130hrs AKL Bihać advised the pilot of the AB.212: 'We've received an order for you to return to Lučko via Ogulin. Therefore, turn 180° back to Lučko, otherwise interceptor aircraft will be sent after you.'

While two MiG-21bis interceptors of the 117th Regiment at Bihać were put on alert for a possible take-off, this proved unnecessary. The Croats confirmed the receipt of the order and flew back to Lučko, arriving there at 1355hrs – much to their luck: their pilots did not know that the RV i PVO knew about the actual purpose of their action and had put two Jastrebs on alert at the Cerklje AB, with the intention of intercepting them.[10]

Despite this failure to reach Knin and re-establish its authority, the government in Zagreb remained persistent, and on 18 August 1990 attempted to reconnoitre the situation in the town. However, the pilot of the Cessna F.172H involved never received permission to take-off. Instead, another Croat pilot then managed to visually reconnoitre Knin after flying his Utva-75 in the radar shadow of Mount Svilaja. A simultaneous attempt on the ground by a column of TAB-71 armoured personnel carriers (APCs) and Land Rovers of the Croatian police to reach the town, was spoiled by multiple roadblocks protected by Serbian militia. The SDS thus managed to retain control and hold a referendum – with a predictable result: close to 100 percent of those who voted, demanded autonomy. As a result, in March 1991 the authorities in most areas of Croatia predominantly populated by the Serbs had declared the establishment of the Serbian Autonomous District (SAO) of Knin's Krajina. The SAO was to form the core of a future Serbian para-state expected to unify all the Serbian-controlled parts of Croatia, with the intention of remaining within the SFRJ.

Following these events, it was obvious that both the Croats and Serbs in Croatia were preparing for war and that an armed conflict was inevitable. The Federal government and the JNA repeatedly appealed for peace, but meanwhile their requests were considered empty phrases of little concern for the dynamics in general, and the development of local paramilitary forces in particular. Indeed, Croatia continued strengthening its police forces, boosting its total complement from 6,800 in mid-1990 to 18,500 in January 1991, and equipping it with dozens of thousands of Kalashnikov assault rifles clandestinely acquired from Hungary. In turn, the Serbs in the SAO Krajina armed themselves with whatever they found in the local stocks of the TO and – through secret channels – from the TO elsewhere. Unknown to most of the population and most of the Federal armed forces, regardless where, the question was no longer *if*, but *when* a war would erupt.

Last-Minute Preparations

As tensions continued to mount, on 9 January 1991 the SIV issued an order for the dissolution of all armed structures outside the chain of command of the unified armed forces of the SFRJ – including all formations established by the local MUPs – within ten days. The government in Zagreb responded that the only illegally armed forces were those in Knin, and then – while handing over symbolic quantities of obsolete armament – mobilised all of its police forces. On 19 January 1991, the deadline for disarmament was extended by 48 hours, but when the Presidency of the SFRJ concluded that the order was only partially executed, on 23 January it requested that all the armed units in the Republic of Croatia be immediately disbanded, threatening to deploy the JNA if not. Indeed, in order to improve the security of major bases, during the night to 24 January, the Jastrebarsko-based 4th Armoured Brigade JNA – equipped with M-84 (an improved, locally designed and manufactured variant of the Soviet T-72 main battle tank, MBT) – deployed its tanks at Pleso International Airport (IAP), while Zemunik, Pula, and Divljue air bases had been prepared for defence. This crisis reached its high point when TV Belgrade aired a documentary prepared by the security authorities of the JNA, about illegal acquisitions of armament for the Croatian police from Hungary. Emotions skyrocketed and there were calls for the apprehending of the Croatian minister of defence. However, just when it looked as if a war was about to erupt at any moment, the crisis slowly faded out. Obviously not satisfied with their current conditions, political leaders in Zagreb and Knin rushed to have the Croatian police and the militia of the SAO Krajina reinforced through additional arms and expanded through the formation of additional units. In particular, and with full support from Milošević, the TO units of the Krajina were bolstered through sizeable arms deliveries. With the Presidency of the SFRJ meanwhile paralysed due to the rivalries between the Serbs, Croats and Slovenes, the next step was undertaken by the SSNO and the General Staff of the JNA: these decided to form the Supreme Command Staff (ŠVK) – a step originally envisaged to be taken only in the case of a war. Effective from the end of January 1991, all the orders issued to the Federal armed forces were by or on behalf of this body.

Final Meeting

On 1 March 1991, Serbian militiamen disarmed Croatian policemen at the police station in Pakrac in western Slavonia. Zagreb reacted by deploying the Lučko anti-terrorist unit – at the time probably the best-trained Croatian unit. The JNA intervened by deploying its troops – supported by Mi-8s of the RV i PVO, and AB.212s of the Federal police – in between the opposing forces.[11] Although a Croatian APC

At a time when the majority of the population was quite certain that the country was facing a civil war, regular training in the JNA continued to be conducted with the focus on defence against sudden aggression. Decades of Cold War left a strong inertia. A symbolic image of that time is the training of coastal artillery in March 1991 at the fortifications on the island of Vis. The technology, a legacy from the Second World War, was a German Flak gun modified into a coastal gun which, according to naval tradition, received a mark made in calibers – D56B2. (Zoran Milovanović, Media Center Odbrana)

Accidental Shooting

The tense atmosphere of the spring of 1991 affected the assessment of pilots and the 252nd Fighter-Bomber Aviation Squadron that they were fired upon on 12 March, when G-4 serial number 23601 was hit while underway over the range off the island of Žirje in the central part of the eastern Adriatic on a target-towing duty. Fired upon by 20mm M71 cannons of Yugoslav Navy minehunters hull numbers LM-153 and LM-161, the crew, Captain 1st Class Brane Majkić and Master-Sergeant Milan Vasić, felt an impact on the airframe and promptly noticed abnormal behaviour of the aircraft, followed by the failure of multiple instruments. Majkić turned back towards Zemunik AB and attempted to eject the target, but the mechanism failed to respond. However, while railing the target in, it fell off into the sea. Using all his experience, the pilot then nursed the badly damaged bird back to the air base, lowered the landing gear and made a safe emergency landing. Post-flight inspection revealed that one round passed between the front and the rear seat in the cockpit, while another damaged not only the target, but also the left drop-tank. An inter-service investigation revealed that it was an accident caused by a series of errors by the crew of LM-161.

In an incident on 12 March 1991 the target tug Galeb-4TM serial 23601 was hit with a 20 mm calibre round from a mine hunter. Works on the repair lasted until February 1992. (Dragan Veličković)

On 13 March 1991 Yugoslav Minister of Defence General Kadijević went to Moscow aboard a Falcon 50 VIP aircraft for an incognito meeting with the last Soviet Minister of Defence, Marshal Dmitry Yazov. (Zdenko Molnar)

The first serious incident in Croatia was the attempt of the Croatian police to enter the town of Pakrac on the night of 1 to 2 March 1991. There were no casualties in the exchange of fire with Serbs leaving the police station. Due to the nature of the incident, on 4 March representatives of the Federal and Croatian authorities and representatives of the JNA and local Serbs came to Pakrac from Belgrade. The Federal Secretary for the Interior Lieutenant-General (retired) Petar Gračanin arrived in an AB.212, which belonged to the air unit of the SSUP. In the evening, when the AB.212 was getting ready for take-off for the return to Belgrade a large number of civilians were in the vicinity of the football field and military police security and a BRDM-2 scout car were posted. (Srđan Ilić)

then opened fire with a machinegun at the Federal troops, the incident ended without casualties.

Nevertheless, Serbian media exploded into reporting that the Croats had 'massacred 40 people' in Pakrac. To say that this created a major public disturbance would be an understatement. Riding the wave of nationalist sentiments, Milošević declared all the other political parties of Serbia to be 'traitors' and 'allies of the Croatian extremists.' In a now well-known fashion, his supporters promptly staged mass demonstrations in Belgrade on 9 March 1991. Since 1987, these demonstrations had usually signalled another political coup in his favour – this time against the Federal authorities. However, a brutal police operation broke up the demonstrations, while the JNA deployed its units on the streets of the Yugoslav capital, clearly demonstrating its determination to preserve the existing order. Indeed, concluding that the political and security conditions were pushing the country straight into a civil war, and in an attempt to prevent this from happening, the ŠVK requested a meeting of the Presidency of the SFRJ.

In a last-ditch attempt to prevent the worst, a series of dramatic sessions was held in Belgrade on 12, 14, and 15 March, during which General Kadijević openly demanded the introduction of a state of emergency and the introduction of a series of decisive and urgent measures to integrate the country's defences into legal frameworks. During the break of the session on 13 March, Kadijević made a major mistake by taking the JRV i PVO's Falcon 50 to travel to Moscow for a meeting with the Soviet Secretary of Defence, Marshal Dmitriy Timofeyevich Yazov, and asking for support. To all too many of proud Yugoslavia, this was the drop that over spilled the barrel: not only that it was shameful for a general of the JNA to ask for Soviet help, but it appeared as if the hardliners within the military were about to launch a coup d'état. Unsurprisingly, the Presidency turned down all the proposals of the ŠVK. For all practical purposes, these three dramatic days signalled the end of the SFRJ and henceforth, even the military leadership was forced into the conclusion that all that was left for it to do was to support those people determined to remain within Yugoslavia, and – peacefully, if possible – break with those who wanted to leave. Later on, Kadijević interpreted this as a decision to protect and defend Serbs living outside Serbia while rallying the JNA within the borders of the reduced Yugoslavia.[12]

3 WAR IN SLOVENIA

While the world-wide public were quite surprised by the outbreak of the war in Slovenia, several months later the first casualties of the civil war in Yugoslavia actually fell on 31 March 1991. Under the cover of fog, early that morning the Croatian police moved into the famous resort of the Plitvice Lakes, where the authorities of the SAO Krajina had removed the Croat managers: in the resulting exchange of small-arms fire, one combatant was killed on each side. Taking this clash seriously, the ŠVK reacted by activating Plan Radan, and ordered the units of the JNA to position themselves as a buffer between the warring parties.

First Clashes in Croatia

While the ground units of the JNA were deploying into selected positions around the SAO Krajina forces, Gazelle helicopters of the RV i PVO could be seen airborne almost all the time and were used to maintain contact between different units. The first into action was a pair of Gazelles from 894th Reconnaissance and Liaison Aviation Squadron, forward deployed at the Slunj testing grounds and assigned to the forward HQ of 5th Military District and IX Corps – both of which were meanwhile prepared for combat operations according to Plan Radan. Following an order issued by the ŠVK on 5 April 1991, the JNA and the RV i PVO prepared for defence in depth

Various armoured and mechanised units of the JNA were concentrated in the wider region of the Plitvice Lakes in 1990, assigned with the task of separating the warring sides. This photograph shows a Polish-manufactured T-55A and Yugoslav-made M-84A MBTs and M-80A IFVs. (Media Center Odbrana)

against an expected attempt of the Croatian police to enter the SAO Krajina-controlled communities of Knin, Benkovac and Obrovac. For this purpose, the air force scheduled Mi-8s from 790th Transport Helicopter Squadron and Gazelles from 895th Reconnaissance and Liaison Aviation Squadron to fly liaison sorties and to support the units subordinated to 5th MD and IX Corps JNA through hauling supplies and ammunition, and evacuating casualties. Moreover, armed helicopters were to provide fire support and fly reconnaissance all around the Lička Plateau and in the regions of Benkovac and Knin. At the time, this order appeared to be just another paper plan. However, there was no denial that the rhetoric of war was entering the JNA's and the RV i PVO's every-day routine.

On 1 May 1991, two Croat police officers were arrested by the Serbian militia in Borovo Selo in Slavonia while trying to pull down the flag of the SFRJ. Pouring fuel on the fire, Zagreb then ordered the Special Police to free the two and a squad sent into Borovo Selo was ambushed on 2 May 1991. Twelve police officers were killed and 21 wounded. This first major clash of the coming war caused widespread outrage amongst Croat nationalists, in turn moving the entire republic irrevocably toward an all-out war of independence. As first, demonstrations were staged in the Dalmatia region, where shops and restaurants recognised as owned by Serbs were destroyed in a series of riots, and one Croatian police officer was murdered. On 7 May 1991, demonstrators in Split murdered a soldier of the JNA. The RV i PVO reacted by cancelling all leave and elevating the combat readiness of its local air bases, especially Zemunik, while the SSNO ordered elements of 10th Motorised Brigade, JNA, from Mostar in Bosnia and Herzegovina into Dalmatia. Early on 7 May 1991, a task force composed of T-55A MBTs and M-60 APCs drove out of its barracks only to run into a roadblock consisting of trucks and coaches erected by ethnic Croats from Široki Brijeg and neighbouring villages. The commander of 10th Motorised Brigade, Colonel Milojko Pantelić, managed to negotiate the safe passage of his unit but the demonstrators continued blocking the road behind it.

On 8 May 1991, the JNA – which assessed that 10th Motorised Brigade was threatened not only by demonstrators, but also by paramilitary forces equipped with automatic assault rifles – requested the Presidency of the SFRJ to authorise an action against this blockade.

Whatever the civilians decided, the ŠVK then issued the order for Operation Skok to be carried out. Eight Mi-8 and Gazelle helicopters of 782nd Helicopter Squadron from Mostar AB, deployed about 250 troops from IV Corps JNA in Sarajevo at four spots behind the blockade in the vicinity of the village of Vranić, while I Battalion of 49th Motorised Brigade, reinforced by a mixed mortar battery and two teams from the JNA's Counter-Sabotage Unit from Pančevo advanced on the ground. Finally, 240th Fighter-Bomber Aviation Squadron from Mostar AB was briefed to provide CAS if necessary. Impressed by this show of force, the demonstrators gave up the blockade but 10th Motorised Brigade was then rerouted to Kupreško polje, an area in the southwest part of Bosnia. Officially at least, the ŠVK announced this was the plan right from the beginning, and that the purpose of its movement was a deployment for the purpose of an exercise. However, it was obvious that this was a mere justification for backing down in the face of public protest.

Meanwhile, tensions remained high in northern Dalmatia, where the village of Kijevo – predominantly populated by Croats – was surrounded by JNA troops. The president of the Croatian Parliament, Vladimir Šeks, demanded to be allowed to visit the place, and the JNA granted permission for a delegation of the Croatian MUP to be flown from Sinj to Kijevo by a Mi-8 of the RV i PVO. However, when the Croats sent their AB.212 (registration YU-HBM) instead, this permission was withdrawn. Rather unsurprisingly, soon after the latter helicopter lifted off from Sinj and approached the Serbian village of Civljani at 1300hrs of 2 May 1991, it attracted strong fire from multiple assault rifles and was hit several times. The crew managed to land safely in the outskirts of Kijevo. After applying emergency repairs, it took off again at around 1900hrs and flew away avoiding the route suggested to it by the JNA out of fear of another ambush.

War Drums

Concluding that open conflict with Croatia was unavoidable, the ŠVK then ordered all the garrisons of the JNA, the RV i PVO, and the RM to prepare for defence from possible attacks. Commanders were authorised to, if necessary, take all defensive precautions, but also to act against republic and local institutions responsible for organising attacks on them. The defence of RV i PVO bases was the responsibility

The last pre-war exercise of the RV i PVO in the western part of the SFRJ was Romanija-91, held from 28 to 31 May 1991 by V Corps RV i PVO. The scenario was of defence from an aggression by NATO and Hungary. The enemy – blue side – was represented by these IJ-21 Oraos, Galeb-2s, and IJ-22 Jastrebs of 352nd Reconnaissance Aviation Squadron, photographed on the tarmac of the Cerklje AB. They simulated an attack by NATO's 5th ATAF (Allied Tactical Air Force). (Zoran Milovanović, Media Center Odbrana)

Lieutenant-General Anton Tus (closest to the camera), who was nearing the end of his career as the commander of the RV i PVO, following a briefing on the course of Exercise Romanija-91 during the last week of May 1991. Sitting beside him was his deputy, Major-General Zvonko Jurjević: Jurjević took over the command of the RV i PVO only a few weeks later. (Krila Armije)

of its own security forces. In addition to the formation of 'infantry companies' – consisting of officers and other ranks of the air force, its military police, and air defence units – personnel from whatever units were available found themselves engaged in defence operations. Henceforth, every garrison in Croatia and Slovenia surrounded itself with minefields and constructed multiple fire positions along its perimeter.

Ironically, while the entire SFRJ was thus clearly sliding into a war, the military bureaucracy remained obsessed with regular assignments and training according its annual planning. Therefore, flying units of the RV i PVO continued their routine exercises. For example, from 28 to 31 May 1991, V Corps of the air force ran Exercise Romanija-91, the scenario of which was based on an aggression by NATO, together with the forces of Hungary and Albania – in reaction to which the RV i PVO was to fly a series of air strikes against, amongst others, a number of air bases in northern Italy. The reason for such activities was that members of the Federal armed forces based in Croatia and Slovenia found themselves facing threats to their personal security and the security of their families. As a constant tension began dominating every-day life, the RV i PVO became keen to maintain an illusion of routine, and thus insisted on continued training for conventional warfare. By doing so, it only played into the hands of its enemies and the media in Slovenia and Croatia reported and presented every single flight by the air force as a provocation and a show of force. Indeed, and keen to prepare the public opinion for the coming war, the Ministries of Information of Croatia and Slovenia claimed that Exercise Romanija-91 was a rehearsal for an all-out attack on the civilian population. While trying to maintain the impression of a strong military force, the RV i PVO vainly attempted to avoid creating a negative image of itself in public. Correspondingly, 107th Mixed Aviation Regiment stopped flying training flights over western Herzegovina because this area was dominated by sympathisers of the HDZ and the even more extreme Croatian Party of Rights (HSP): instead, it flew its training sorties over eastern Herzegovina, where the Serbs formed the majority of the population.

Multi-Ethnic Command Structure

On 14 June 1991, the Commander of the JRV i PVO, Colonel-General Anton Tus, handed over his position to Lieutenant-General Zvonko Jurjević, an experienced flight instructor and the former chief of the Air Force Academy. Jurjević and his new deputy, Major-General Živan Mirčetić (a former MiG-21 pilot) were both representatives of a hard-line pro-SFRJ group of officers that was about to play a crucial role during the coming war.[1] At the time, the composition of the RV i PVO – and indeed, that of the JNA in particular – was still multinational, and the pro-Yugoslav positions still had a firm foothold within the commands of all the branches. The units deployed in the western SFRJ especially were still staffed following the model of 'brotherhood and unity': the commander of V Corps JRV i PVO, for example, was Major-General Marijan Rožič, a Slovene; his deputy was Colonel Ljubomir Bajić, a Serb. Similarly, the commander of 82nd Aviation Brigade was Lieutenant-Colonel Jožef Jerič, a Slovene; 111th Aviation Brigade was under the command of Colonel Andrija Veselinović, a Croat; and 117th Fighter Aviation Regiment was commanded by Lieutenant-Colonel Mahmut Skadrak, who declared himself as a Serb.[2]

Croatian National Guard

The Croats were also busy training and re-shuffling their personnel, but for more realistic purposes – and there is also little doubt that both the leaders in Zagreb and in Ljubljana were in possession of much more realistic estimates about the number of military professionals still serving in the Federal armed forces but likely to switch sides. On 28 May 1991, the government in Zagreb officially established the Croatian National Guard (Zbor Nacionalne Garde, ZNG). Initially, the ZNG was subjected to the jurisdiction of the Ministry of Interior and its manoeuvre elements consisted of four brigades with just 2,000 trained officers and other ranks. However, this was rather unsurprising during this transitional period, the nascent armed forces of Croatia were a heterogenous hodgepodge of police and (future) military forces, some with excellent training (up to the level of anti-terrorist operations), others with a bare minimum of training in use of their firearms. Moreover, the ultra-right-wing Croatian Party of Rights (HSP) established its own paramilitary wing designated the Croatian Defence Forces (HOS), which was to play an important role during the early stages of the Yugoslav Wars – both in Croatia, and in Bosnia and Herzegovina.

War Atmosphere in Slovenia

As described above, Slovenia was politically and media-wise preparing for the declaration of independence from at least early 1990. A year later, its TOS was estimated at having enough weapons to arm about 40,000 officers and other ranks. The core consisted of around 5,000 troops under the age of 25, equipped with modern infantry arms and anti-tank rockets, and organised into seven regional headquarters designated 2nd, 3rd, 4th, 5th, 6th, 7th, and the 8th, and the 30th Development Group, a special purpose unit.[3]

Between 22 and 24 March 1991, the TOS units carried out Exercise Premik, designed to follow a realistic scenario of mobilisation and a battle with the JNA. During this exercise, the Slovenes trained for taking control over their borders, and blocking the movement of enemy ground forces by the means of barriers and roadblocks. On 13 May 1991, the TOS issued a report to the Slovenian government, according to which the force reported being equipped with 99 anti-aircraft guns, and 42 Strela-2M MANPADS.

The RV i PVO was meanwhile also preparing for possible action in Slovenia. Major Vinko Tuljak, assistant commander of 351st Reconnaissance Aviation Squadron, recalled being ordered to fly his IJ-22 Orao on sorties over Kočevski Rog and Kočevska Reka, which served as major bases of the TOS. He recalled that neither him, nor his colleague Captain 1st Class Marjan Penev, was able to accomplish the mission: the installation angle of their cameras, and the large altitude difference of the mountainous terrain made it impossible to take photographs from low altitude. Instead, they flew their missions at high altitude, taking wide-angle photographs, each of which covered 25 by 20 kilometres – which they knew would be useless in the event of an attack on Slovenia. Furthermore, Tuljak recalled that on 15 March 1991, the commander of 351st Squadron, Major Đino Vareško, ordered six of his pilots to prepare for low-altitude flyovers of all the larger towns of Slovenia, with the aim of intimidating the population, an order they were to keep secret from the rest of the unit. But, 'in my head, I kept repeating data for Graz airport: radio-navigational means, the direction of the runway, procedure for approach and landing' – recalled Tuljak, who was seriously contemplating a defection. Once, while he was studying his possible escape route, Penev suddenly entered the office – only to open the navigation chart showing southern Austria: they were both thinking the same.

First Clashes in Slovenia

As the tensions between the JNA and the TOS continued to rise, the Slovenes went into action. On 23 May 1991, the guards of the 710th Training Centre in Pekre, outside Maribor – used to take up and train novice recruits assigned to the TOS instead to the JNA – apprehended a number of JNA troops who attempted to take a closer look. The Federals were released, shortly after, but then the JNA deployed six BRDM-2 and M86 armoured vehicles to block the entry to Pekre. When the two sides entered negotiations in Maribor, the Military Police of the JNA intervened and arrested Lieutenant-Colonel Vladimir Milošević, commander of 7th Regional HQ, TOS, one of his officers and two bodyguards of a Slovenian official. The Slovenes reacted by protesting down the streets of Maribor for the following two days, and then cut off the telephone links and electricity for the local base of the JNA. By tapping telephone cables, their intelligence service then learned that the JNA intended to transfer Milošević to Zagreb. Ljubljana thus issued the order to intercept the helicopter that was to pick him up by the means of several suitably positioned anti-aircraft guns: the Slovenians are convinced that due to this deployment, not only was Milošević's transfer suspended, but he was even released.[4]

Lifting Kragujs

Following an SSNO decision from 1975, each of the six TOs in the constituent republics of Yugoslavia was to form one squadron that was, in the case of an emergency, supposed to make use of aircraft usually operated by civilian aero clubs, or that were privately owned. Their pilots included a mix of reservists and civilians with pilot licences, all of whom underwent additional training at the School of Reserve Aviation of the VVA, at Tuzla AB. After this course, civilian pilots received the rank of '2nd Lieutenant, Reserve.' From 1977 until 1988, the resulting units were equipped with a mix of 12 Utva-66 liaison aircraft and Soko J-20 Kraguj light piston-engined strikers and

The flight line of 129th FAS at Pula on 6 June 1991, a couple of weeks before pilots from the unit took off on their first combat assignments in Slovenia with MiG-21PFMs and MiG-21UMs. (Aleksandar Radić)

Pilots of the Slovenian TO's aviation, after the last pre-war exercise completed on 20 May 1990. The aircraft were under the control of the JNA on the military part of Brnik airport. (Peter Merljak)

While considered a 'real combat aircraft', the Kraguj possessed only modest performance. Powered by a US-made Lycoming GSO-480B1A6 engine with a maximum output of 340hp, it had a normal take-off weight of around 1,600kgs, and a maximum speed of only 210km/h. It was armed with two 7.7mm machineguns and had only two underwing pylons for bombs or rocket pods, and two launch rails for 5-inch HVAR rockets. (Miha Kos via Tomaž Perme)

counterinsurgency (COIN) fighters. Starting in 1989, the reservists were re-qualified to fly G-2 Galebs and 12 surviving Kragujs were assigned to the Slovenian TO and seven to the Montenegrin TO. Encouraged to fly as often as possible, Slovenian reservists took their duties very seriously, and flew regularly – including several live firing exercises at one of the local training ranges.

In 1990, the commander of the Slovenian squadron that operated Kragujs, Peter Merljak, established contact with the command of the TOS, and plotted a plan to remove all 12 aircraft from Brnik. However, this idea proved unrealistic because all the tools for their maintenance and all their weaponry were stored at Cerklje AB, out of the reach of the TOS. By coincidence, when in May 1990 the ŠVK arrived at the decision to hand over all the stored heavy armament of the Slovenian TO to Ljubljana, the Kragujs and their pilots were on temporary redeployment to Cerklje AB, on an exercise. All were promptly flown back to Brnik but put under the guard of the JNA. Things were to remain that way until early June 1991 when, understanding that an armed conflict with Slovenia was imminent and the TOS was likely to try securing the Kragujs, the ŠVK and the RV i PVO decided to transfer them, 'somewhere east'. Obviously, with Slovenian independence approaching, this was a particularly sensitive issue and the risk of a clash with the Slovenian police, which was guarding the airport, was considered high. The task had to be carried out 'in silence'. The RV i PVO collected six pilots from 252nd Fighter-Bomber Aviation Squadron at Batajnica, and – from 10 until 13 June – rushed them through a refresher course on the Kragujs of the Montenegrin TO, which also provided additional pilots. Early on 21 June, two Mi-8s from 780th Transport Helicopter Squadron then took off from Cerklje AB, carrying elements of the Commando Detachment of 65th Protection Motorised Regiment, while 14th Battalion Military Police was deployed around Brnik IAP. A pair of J-21s armed with 5-inch HVAR rockets provided top cover. On landing, commandos of the Sabotage Detachment rushed out of the first helicopter, followed by pilots and technicians out of the second and in the course of an operation that lasted only 20 minutes all 10 Kragujs present at Brnik were flown out to Cerklje, where they joined the other two that were already there for maintenance purposes. Later on, all 12 Kragujs were flown to Bihać AB, then to Tuzla, and finally to Batajnica AB. After being handed over to 252nd Fighter-Bomber Aviation Squadron for maintenance, five were transferred to the Montenegrin TO.[5]

Meanwhile, three Gazelles of 2nd Flight from 894th Reconnaissance and Liaison Aviation Squadron remained at Brnik IAP, and one of their pilots, Captain 1st Class Jože Kalan, was ordered to fly reconnaissance of 30th Development Group's base in Kočevska Reka. Kalan – accompanied by an officer from 14th Mixed Artillery Regiment based in Ribnica and his bodyguard – then flew his mission. During the following days, Brnik-based 2nd Flight of 894th Reconnaissance and Liaison Aviation Squadron was transferred to the JNA's base in Šentvid outside Ljubljana.[6]

Slovenian Independence

By the last week of June 1991, the Slovenian political decision to leave the SFRJ became irreversible. On the 24th of the month, Ljubljana ordered a mobilisation of the TOS, and a day later parliaments of both Slovenia and Croatia adopted the declaration of sovereignty and independence. Although in a shock, the Federal authorities promptly declared all such announcements to be null and void: in particular, they opposed the Slovenian decision to secure control over all of the international border crossings and establish border crossings to Croatia. With the president of the SIV, Marković, imposing a ban on erection of border crossings inside the SFRJ, the General Staff of the JNA and the Federal law enforcement authorities in Belgrade had no other solution than to prepare a joint operation against such an act. Of course, all of the related planning and the execution were to be directed by the ŠVK. In turn, the officers there expected no resistance from the Slovenes and that the crisis would be resolved through peaceful negotiations. Drawing on experiences from the events in Kosmet in 1988, the ŠVK thus ordered the deployment of only about 1,900 troops from various units of 5th MD JNA. These were to operate in small, widely dispersed groups, deemed sufficient to intimidate the Slovenes while offering sufficient protection to the involved troops. They were to secure conditions for a heliborne deployment of a brigade of the Federal Police and Custom Services, with help of Mi-8s from 780th Transport Helicopter Squadron. Finally, Jastrebs and Oraos from Cerklje AB were to make low altitude passes in a show of force. However, from the point of view of the Slovenian authorities, the issue of securing border crossings was critical for the independence of this republic from the SFRJ. Correspondingly, all the 15,707 mobilised members of the TOS were put on alert and ordered to deploy around strategically important installations.

Early Chaos

Under the original plan of the ŠVK, the JNA and the Federal police were supposed to secure all the border crossings by 1400hrs of 26 June 1991. Correspondingly, early on 26 June, a Mi-8 helicopter carrying three forward air controllers (FACs) arrived at the JNA base in Šentvid. During the afternoon, it was followed by six additional Mi-8s, carrying members of the Commando Detachment. However, the ŠVK then changed its mind and postponed all the related movements to a day later, with a deadline of 1500hrs on 27 June. Moreover, the commander of XIII Corps JNA, Lieutenant-General Marijan Čad, then ordered his units to move out from their base in Ilirska Bistrica, and thus on 26 June 1991, eleven T-55 MBTs, six M36 tank destroyers, three BRDM-2 scout cars, two M86 armoured vehicles, and one infantry company went out to secure the border crossing of Sežana (crossing to Trieste in Italy). The, order was carried out by 1900hrs, without the use of force – ironically around the same time the Slovenian government and a mass of civilians were celebrating their independence on the main square in Ljubljana. When the festivities were disturbed by the appearance of several MiGs, the Slovenian Minister of Defence, Janez Janša, made a call to the commander of V Corps RV i PVO, Major-General Rožič and threatened to open fire. Unknown to the Federal armed forces, Janša next initiated Operation Kamen: a plan to block all the major routes used by the JNA for movement through Slovenia. Knowing the threat was serious because the TOS has acquired several Strela-2Ms a few days earlier, Janša phoned Rožič and said he would order the TOS troops to open fire and shoot down the aircraft. This is how the JRV i PVO went into its first – and its fateful last – war.

Into the War

Shortly after midnight of 26 to 27 June 1991, multiple JNA units – including a total of 122 combat vehicles of XIV, XXXI, and XXXII Corps, and the air defence battalion of 580th Mixed Artillery Brigade

The military part of Brnik Airport where the flight from the Gazelle-equipped 894th Reconnaissance and Liaison Aviation Squadron used to be stationed. Until the flyover on 21 June 1991, J-20 Kraguj light attack aircraft were on the flight line. (Tomaž Mrlak collection)

Gazelle serial 12664 was permanently stationed at Brnik airport from 1981 to support the needs of the land forces commands in the territory of Slovenia. Pilot Anton Mrlak was shot down in this Gazelle on 27 June 1991. (Tomaž Mrlak collection)

(a unit directly subordinated to HQ 5th MD), drove out of their bases and headed for nearest border crossings in columns, as follows:

- from Varaždin (in Croatia) via Ormož for Gornja Radgona (crossing to Bad Radkersburg in Austria)
- from Maribor for Šentilj (crossing to Spielfeld in Austria)
- from Karlovac (in Croatia) for Ljubljana and Jesenice (southern entry to the Karawanks Tunnel to Austria)
- from Vrhnika for Brnik IAP, and
- from Postojna via Ajdovščina for Nova Gorica (crossing to Gorizia in Italy)

The plan of the JNA for control of the border was primarily based on the concept of a force that was supposed to intimidate the Slovenian TO and citizens and therefore armoured vehicles were used for the mission. It was expected that the armour would protect soldiers from potential incidents, however, they found themselves under fire and faced a choice whether to be destroyed or to surrender. The crew of the T-55A, serial 19625, from 195th Motorised Brigade, handed over its tank to the TOS. (J. Andanson)

Most of the columns of the JNA found their way blocked by extensive roadblocks – often within minutes of exiting their bases – well positioned within countless bottlenecks along the winding roads of Slovenia and erected as a part of Operation Kamen, these consisted of dozens of trucks (often filled with sand) and coaches, protected by TOS troops cleared to fire. Whenever a JNA column approached one of the barricades, it was forced to stop and then repeatedly subjected to disruptive fire by the Slovenes while trying to punch through or to find a way around the roadblock. Unsurprisingly, by the dawn of 27 June, the Federals had failed to reach any of the border crossings. Instead, in a shock, the Federal officers found their units isolated and fighting for survival: most proved to be indecisive, indeed passive, and refusing to launch a determined attack.

Nevertheless, still expecting no resistance and slow to realise what was actually going on, the ŠVK meanwhile ordered the operation to continue as planned. Early in the morning, several reconnaissance aircraft launched from Cerkje AB. For example, Lieutenant-Colonel Jerič, an experienced Jastreb and Orao pilot of 82nd Attack Brigade, flew no less than four sorties on both IJ-21s and IJ-22s that day, including reconnaissance of the border crossings and various TOS bases (such as their training centres in Pekre and Ig).[7] The diary of 252nd Fighter Bomber Aviation Squadron also registered the first operational sortie ever flown by this unit on 27 June 1991. At 1000hrs, five An-26s and a single Yak-40 were to take off from Batajnica AB, carrying 361 Federal police officers and 270 Customs officers to Cerklje AB, where they were awaited by 19 Mi-8 helicopters. However, the organisation of this part of the enterprise proved poor: amid great confusion, officers and other ranks wearing their summer uniforms were issued assault rifles and ordered to embark An-26 transport aircraft, without any kind of information about what was expected from them. After several delays, the aircraft reached Cerklje AB only around 1200hrs and the officers were then quickly transferred to the helicopters, and these launched at 1245hrs.

Methodical Procedure for closing Border Crossings

Regardless – or precisely because – of a tightly centralised command and control structure of the Yugoslav armed forces, the chaos within the ranks of the JNA, the RV i PVO, and the Federal police, only increased once the Mi-8s were underway towards their targets. Never informed about the threat of Strela-2Ms, and not equipped with any kind of self-protection measures, they flew at 'peace-time altitudes' of several hundred meters, only to find themselves exposed to all sorts of ground fire. Things didn't get better once they attempted to land near selected border crossings: ground troops of the JNA were nowhere to be seen, there was no supportive fire and landing spots were poorly selected – while the TOS was not only on full alert, and in position, but shooting back with all available means. Perhaps the worst experience of the day was that of one Mi-8-crew tasked with deploying Federal police officers to the southern entry of the Karawanks Tunnel. Jerič later recalled that the paratrooper officer in command of this operation ordered all 80 of his troops to embark the Mi-8s at once and requested CAS from 82nd Aviation Brigade. Jerič forwarded that request to HQ V Corps RV i PVO but was told not to carry out the mission. Furious, the para disembarked most of his troops and went on nevertheless. On approach to the target zone, one of the Mi-8s was hit by multiple bullets, one of which wounded the flight technician, and another one of the police officers. A video clip subsequently aired by TV Politika in Belgrade showed a clear trail of machine gun fire from a BOV-M of the TOS.[8] Deploying reinforcements to this zone was possible only after sunset. After landing at a nearby football field the police officers did then manage to secure the border crossing.

Operating from Šentvid, 2nd Flight of 894th Reconnaissance and Liaison Aviation Squadron was in action the entire day. Kalan recalled that after flying visual reconnaissance along the road from Ljubljana to Novo Mesto and from Ljubljana to Celje, he was tasked with flying to Maribor in support of the units of XXXI Corps. During this first sortie there, he deployed two officers from the HQ of that Corps to a tank column blocked outside Ormoz and his passengers handed over a sealed envelope with orders to the local commander before

Paratroopers at War

Although the defenders of the various RV i PVO air bases in Slovenia and Croatia were firmly holding their positions, on 26 June the ŠVK ordered that they be reinforced by elements of 63rd Parachute Brigade – not only the elite of the RV i PVO, but the entire JNA. These were deployed by An-26s from their home-base in Niš to their destinations the day that the order was issued in what were the first ever operational assignments of this unit. The original purpose of 63rd Parachute Brigade was comparable to that of the Special Air Service (SAS) in Great Britain: commando operations in the enemy rear. Correspondingly, its two parachute infantry companies, two parachute commando companies, and a parachute reconnaissance platoon – all staffed by professional soldiers – were only lightly armed. However, during the war, the ŠVK regularly deployed them for operations of 'aggressive defence' of the major air bases of the RV i PVO in Croatia and Slovenia. On 27 June, even troops not assigned any tasks – and indeed considered 'surplus' by their superiors – embarked aboard An-26s that flew to Cerklje AB. Ignoring any kind of division along ethnic lines, the paras all volunteered to go into action because of their devotion to duty and were to demonstrate particularly fierce combat spirit in the following days.[10]

The home-base of 63rd Parachute Brigade was Niš, where the An-26s of 677th Squadron were based. Early during the war the paratroopers were provided with M-89 camouflage uniforms instead of the usual olive-drab ones. (Ivan Detiček Collection)

embarking again. The next stop was at Murska Sobota: immediately after taking-off from there, Kalan saw a firefight that erupted on the ground. His final flight of the day was to the Sunjak border post, from where he evacuated a wounded corporal of the JNA to the hospital in Maribor.[9] However, perhaps the most absurd example of the day was when the HQ 5th Corps tasked the Gazelle-crews with the distribution of a 'suitably' titled manual, 'Methodical Procedure for closing Border Crossings'

Meanwhile, Utva-66 aircraft were deployed to drop over 100,000 leaflets over all the major urban centres of Slovenia urging the population to comply with the decisions of the Federal authorities. Between 1600 and 1700hrs, two Mi-8 helicopters landed at a football field outside Dravograd and disembarked 15 troops of 115th Anti-Sabotage Company. Alerted before their arrival, 8th Regional HQ TSO deployed its units into blocking positions and, as soon as the helicopters were away, surrounded the stadium. The commander of the Federal unit was promptly ordered to surrender and shocked by the fact that he had been deployed in Ormoz instead at the border post at Vič the officer gave up without further discussion. However, only 13 of his troops were taken captive: two others managed to escape to the JNA base in Bukovje. Slightly more successful were subsequent operations: at 1700hrs two Mi-8s landed 36 troops and two 82mm recoilless guns at the border crossing of Hodoš and two hours later these were reinforced by another 19 Federal Police and Customs officers.

Meanwhile, all the An-26s from 679th Transport Aviation Squadron (part of 138th Brigade) were transferred from Pleso to Batajnica AB. The needs for airlift were great for a limited fleet that was maintaining an air bridge between Cerklje and bases in the east of SFRJ.

Tanks at Brnik IAP

As well as deploying paratroopers and Federal Police and Customs officers in accordance with the ŠVK's plan, crews of Gazelle and Mi-8 helicopters were tasked with several ad-hoc sorties, mostly including the deployment of reinforcements. One such operation was undertaken in support of I Battalion, 1st Armoured Brigade JNA, tanks of which were supposed to secure Brnik IAP. The unit moved out of its base in Vrhnika at 0230hrs of 27 June, organised in two columns:

- The 'right', with 10 M-84 MBTs, 6 M-80A IFVs, and one BTR-50PU APC, travelled from Vrhnika around Ljubljana to Trzin and Moste in attempt to reach Brnik from the south-east, while
- the 'left' with 10 M-84s and 5 M-80As, took a direct route from Vrhnika to the airport.

This photograph was taken from a Mi-8 helicopter during a flyover above the barracks of 1st Armored Brigade in Vrhnika and shows the combat equipment of a unit that had one of the primary roles in the intervention in Slovenia – M-84 MBTs and M-80A IFVs, PT-76B reconnaissance tanks, and various tracked and wheeled vehicles for recovery and logistics. (Mladen Savić)

After passing Ljubljana, the right column ran into a barricade in Trzin, west of Domžale: while searching for a way around the obstacle one of its M-80As had its tracks damaged, and two IFVs had to be left behind for its protection. A few kilometres later, while passing the village of Moste, the same column then lost an M-84 that suffered technical problems. Nevertheless, both columns managed to reach their destination and secure the airport – but not before Slovenian pilots evacuated one AB.412 (registration YU-HCX), one AB.212 (YU-HCJ), one Agusta A.109A (YU-HBN), and two AB.206B Jet Ranger IIIs (YU-HCV and YU-HCW) of the Slovenian police to Gotenica, near Kočevje, close to the Croatian border. There, the helicopters remained hidden for the rest of the war. Back at Brnik, I Battalion of 1st Armoured Brigade established a perimeter defence of the crucial installation, with 15 M-84s, 7 remaining M-80As, and the sole BTR-50PU all deployed around the runway, south of the airport, and facing in the southern direction. Around 1500hrs, the battalion was reinforced by 15 Police and Customs officers deployed by a single Mi-8.

Meanwhile, both sides scrambled to get the M-84 and three M-80As that had been left behind. The TOS deployed a tank-hunting team equipped with 16 Armbrusts and reinforced by a unit of the Special Militia Unit (SEM), while the JRV i PVO deployed multiple helicopters. Of course, the latter were quicker: shortly after a Gazelle evacuated the M-84's crew, the civilians removed everything they could dismantle from the tank and then set it on fire. The ensuing combustion of the ammunition then ripped the turret away. Around 1451hrs, a Gazelle from 894th Squadron landed next to the three M-80s to supply the troops with dry rations and water. The TOS troops arrived around 1800hrs and promptly attacked Brnik IAP. They damaged the BTR-50PU and wounded six officers and one soldier, prompting the commander of 1st Armoured Brigade to personally embark a Mi-8 helicopter at Vrhnika, and fly in to Brnik to supervise their evacuation.

A major clash followed about half an hour later, when the TOS attempted to attack the three M-80As left behind in Trzin. Shortly after, two Mi-8s arrived to disembark 27 troops of the Sabotage Detachment: the latter opened fire at the approaching Slovenes while the helicopters carrying them were about to land, and the TOS retaliated by firing two Armbrusts: one misfired, while the other missed the target. Emboldened, the crews of the M-80As then opened fire with their automatic cannon: sandwiched between the IFVs and commandos, the Slovenian tank-hunters quickly lost one soldier killed and were forced to withdraw. The SEM then solved the

Remains of the Mi-8 shot down on 27 June 1991. In the foreground, a launcher for 57mm unguided rockets can clearly be seen. In the background is the leg of the main landing gear and parts of the burnt fuselage. (Tanjug)

Remains of downed Gazelle 12664 recorded moments after the fall, while still on fire. (Tomaž Mrlak collection)

After a long period of growing crisis, the civil war in the SFRJ began brutally. The loaves of bread that were being carried by the Gazelle crewed by Mrlak and Sibinovski were a potent image of the atmosphere at that time. (Tomaž Mrlak collection)

crisis by damaging two M-80As and killing three JNA troops. Encircled, the landing party and the surviving crews surrendered to the Slovenes on the next day.

The Loss of Two Helicopters

Through all of this time, the Coordination Group of the Slovenian Ministries of Interior and Defence – staffed by well-qualified people, including the commander of the TOS, all directly responsible to the president of the republic – cautiously controlled the battle. Realising that the key role in the movement of the JNA troops was played by helicopters – which proved capable of quickly bypassing barricades – they issued an order for the TOS to open fire at any of the helicopters passing by, regardless of their position, and using whatever means were available. Their troops found suitable opportunities sooner than expected.

At 1830hrs, Mi-8 serial number 12408 from 780th Transport Helicopter Squadron took off from Cerklje AB carrying supplies to one of the military bases outside the Slovenian capitol. On the way back, the helicopter crewed by Captain 1st Class Milenko Jorgić (35), Lieutenant Eldin Hrapović (26), and technician Master Sergeant Miroslav Šandor (35), returned towards Cerklje flying at an altitude of only 300 metres. At 1900, while flying over the 510th Training Centre of the TOS outside the village of Ig, it came under small-arms fire. Reporting to flight control, Jorgić was ordered to turn around and return fire with 57mm unguided rockets. The crew confirmed the receipt of that order, but shortly afterwards the helicopter was hit by a single Strela-2M, and promptly shot down, killing everybody on board. Jerič recalled: 'I was listening on the radio in my office [to] the conversation of helicopter crews

Based at Cerklje AB, Mi-8s of 780th Transport Helicopter Squadron – including the example 12406 shown here – were some of the first machines of the RV i PVO to see action during the war in Slovenia. On 27 June, they transported paratroopers of 63rd Parachute Brigade and Federal Police and Customs officers to the international border crossings to Austria and Italy. Initially unarmed, because of expectations that there would be no threat, later the same day they began deploying Soviet-made UB-16-57 pods for 57mm S-5K unguided rockets. Another helicopter from the batch was 12408, shot down late on 27 June 1991. As of 1991, the entire Mi-8 fleet of the RV i PVO was painted in grey-green overall, with undersurfaces of the cabin and the boom in light blue. (Artwork by Tom Cooper)

The Yugoslav designation for the SA.342L equipped for anti-tank operations was HN-45M Gama. As of July 1991, the example with serial number 12924 was one of only five serving with 713th Anti-Tank Helicopter Squadron – the smallest unit of the RV i PVO. Four of these were HN-45Ms, while one was the 'utility' H-45 version. Ultimately, this unit was planned to receive its full complement of 17, as 711th Squadron, based at nearby Pleso. Due to the crisis, 713th Squadron moved to Pleso and then to Bihać, until it was disbanded and integrated into 711th Anti-Tank Helicopter Squadron on 6 October 1991. All the Gazelles of the JRV i PVO were painted in glossy grey-green overall: they had tactical numbers and type designation on the cabin (together with the airframe number, No. 138 in this case), roundels and the full serial on the boom, the type's nick-name and the national tricolour on the fin. The Gama helicopters carried four Malytka anti-tank guided missiles (NATO AT-3 Sagger) and two Strela-2M air-to-air missiles. This configuration was only ever seen at air shows however and during the civil war there were no aerial targets and therefore Strela-2M missiles were not mounted. (Artwork by Tom Cooper)

During the crises in Croatia and Slovenia in 1990 and 1991, Gazelles of the RV i PVO appeared to be omnipresent and were seen by civilians on a daily basis. The reason was that the type was intensively deployed for reconnaissance, for liaison, and also VIP-transport purposes, and flew very low – often along main roads, and frequently between buildings. Serial number 12718 was an SA.341H: a HI-42 Hera of 894th Reconnaissance and Liaison Aviation Squadron, a unit that had three Gazelles forward deployed at Brnik IAP in June 1991 and primarily served the command of XIV Corps JNA. (Artwork by Tom Cooper)

The only medium transport type in service with the RV i PVO was the An-26B, 15 of which were available as of June 1991. Two were undergoing overhauls, seven served with 679th Transport Aviation Squadron at Pleso, and six with 677th Transport Aviation Squadron at Niš. From the beginning of the crisis in Slovenia, most were concentrated at Batajnica AB, which became the main hub for airlift operations. Eventually, all the aircraft from Pleso – including the example shown here, serial number 71385 – were transferred to Serbia and 677th Squadron maintained a permanent detachment of four, then six aircraft at Batajnica, while all others were concentrated at Niš. During the fighting of 1991, Yugoslav An-26s flew a total of 902 sorties. The entire fleet wore the same camouflage pattern applied in dark sea grey (BS381C/638) and dark green (BS381C/641) on top surfaces and sides, and PRU blue on undersurfaces. (Artwork by Tom Cooper)

On 28 June, 105th Fighter-Bomber Aviation Regiment carried out its first combat assignment from Zemunik AB. The first jet to take-off was this G-4 Super Galeb, serial number 23727, from 249th Fighter-Bomber Aviation Squadron, armed with a pair of L128-04MD pods for 128mm unguided rockets (inboard pylons) and carrying two 350-litre drop tanks (outboard pylons). M74 (HE warhead) and M-80 (HEAT warhead) unguided rockets were deployed in large numbers during the wars in Slovenia and then in Croatia, but for operations over Slovenia, usually only two or three were loaded per launcher, to lessen the total weight of the aircraft and thus extend the range. 249th Squadron later moved to Udbina AB, where it was much closer to most of the battlefields in Croatia. (Artwork by Tom Cooper)

As of the summer of1991, the mass of visual reconnaissance and power-demonstration sorties over Croatia were assigned to units flying the J-21 Jastreb, a light striker armed with three internally installed 12.7mm Browning M3 machine guns in the nose. Underwing hardpoints enabled the installation of a total of two 100kg or 250kg bombs and up to six 5-inch HVAR (5in/127mm) unguided rockets. J-21 serial number 24130 was assigned to Mostar-based 240th Fighter-Bomber Aviation Squadron at the time, and is shown as armed with a L57-17MD pod for 57mm S-5K unguided rockets: this was the – shorter – Yugoslav variant of the ubiquitous Soviet-made UB-16-57 pod, which was sometimes carried without its aerodynamic front cover, for quicker re-load. While involved in routine exercises in August, this unit flew regular combat sorties in September 1991, and was not only one of the first to remove the large white tactical numbers from the noses of its jets, but also one where this work was done with particular care. (Artwork by Tom Cooper)

238th Fighter-Bomber Aviation Squadron at Cerklje was the first unit to convert to J-22 Oraos in 1985. During the war in Slovenia, many of its personnel quit and on 27 June 1991 its aircraft were evacuated to Pleso, then to Bihać, and finally to Banja Luka, from where it began flying combat sorties on 11 August 1991. This artwork shows the aircraft equipped with the L-57-16MD pod for 57mm S-5K unguided rockets on the inboard underwing pylon and the L-128-04MD pod for 128mm unguided rockets on the outboard underwing pylon. On 5 September, Captain Alija Huskić flew this jet – serial number 25116 – on a reconnaissance sortie over Croatia. On return to base, due to fatigue, he forgot to lower the landing gear and made a belly landing. The aircraft was subsequently repaired at the Moma Stanojlović Works, while Huskić changed his 'Muslim' name to Aleksa Vuković. He continued flying Oraos until killed in an accident on 18 June 1995. (Artwork by Tom Cooper)

351st Reconnaissance Aviation Squadron from Cerklje was heavily tasked during the wars in Slovenia and Croatia. Standard equipment of its IJ-22s (early variant, with engines without afterburners, re-purposed for reconnaissance tasks) consisted of a large centreline-installed pod carrying five A-39 and one AShChAFA-5M Soviet-made cameras, and a British made ICLS-401 infra-red line-scanner. Development of an advanced pod containing Vinten 753A and 880 cameras was cancelled due to the outbreak of the war. This aircraft flew several dozen reconnaissance sorties over Slovenia and Croatia until being handed over to 353rd Reconnaissance Aviation Squadron in Mostar. Like all indigenously manufactured fighter-bombers, all Oraos of the RV i PVO wore a standardised camouflage pattern in dark sea grey (BS381C/638) and dark green (BS381C/641) on upper surfaces and sides, and PRU blue on undersurfaces. (Artwork by Tom Cooper)

The lack of supersonic multi-role aircraft prompted the RV i PVO to compensate through the deployment of MiG-21bis for battlefield interdiction and CAS purposes. Correspondingly, during the second half of the 1980s, MiG-21bis pilots of 117th Fighter Aviation Regiment were re-trained for ground attack, and their aircraft adapted to deploy British-made Hunting BL.755 CBUs, some 4,500 of which were acquired. During the war in Slovenia, 117th Regiment kept a flight of four MiG-21bis from 125th Fighter Aviation Squadron on alert, all armed with BL.755s. One of these was serial number 17210, which originally served with 204th Fighter Aviation Regiment before being handed over to 125th Squadron/117th Regiment. As usual for Yugoslav MiG-21bis, it was painted in 'air superiority grey' overall, wore the roundels in four positions, serials also in four positions, and the large national tricolour across the fin. Notable is the patch of the Zmaj Works, applied near the top of the fin on all aircraft that had been overhauled there. (Artwork by Tom Cooper)

During the fourth year of their curriculum at the VVA, future fighter pilots of the RV i PVO underwent a conversion to supersonic jets while flying MiG-21UMs and MiG-21PFMs of 129th Fighter Aviation Squadron at Pula AB. Permanent personnel of this unit consisted of experienced flight instructors: unsurprisingly, they became involved in combat operations in Slovenia and then Croatia right from the start. One of the much-favoured jets of the squadron was MiG-21PFM serial number 22705, which instead of its original R11F2S-300 (MM14), was powered by the slightly more powerful R11F2SK-300 (MM-15) engine. This jet was also involved in the interception of the Boeing 707 carrying arms for Croats on 31 August 1991, in the configuration as shown here including one R-3S air-to-air missile under each wing, and the GP-9 gun-pod for 23mm GSh-23 gun under the centreline. Notable is Zmaj-applied, highly polished aluminium overall colour, which replaced the originally applied mix of aluminium powder and clear lacquer. (Artwork by Tom Cooper)

During the 1980s, the JNA intended to solve its chronic lack of ability to collect intelligence from the depth of surrounding countries by acquiring Northrop RF-5E Tiger Eye reconnaissance fighters from the USA. Lack of funding prevented the realisation of this plan and instead the Yugoslavs then acquired Fairchild Weston (now part of BAE Systems) KA-112A Long Range Aerial Photography (LORAP) cameras. With the help of Messerschmitt-Bölkow-Blohm (now part of Airbus), these were adapted for carriage in an oversized pod, the installation of which required further modifications on the rear lower fuselages of four MiG-21MFs (L-15Ms). The four jets were heavily utilised all through 1991, flying a total of 28 sorties during the month, 12 of these by the example shown here, serial number 22867. All MiG-21MFs equipped with the LORAP-pod wore the finish in aluminium overall, and the usual set of markings. (Artwork by Tom Cooper)

Between 1989 and August 1990, the Zmaj Works received 20 Iraqi AF MiG-21bis for overhaul, of which 12 had been completed when the works on the remaining examples were suspended due to the UN-imposed arms embargo against Iraq. With the situation in the Zagreb area reaching boiling point, in early July 1991 three intact jets – all originally manufactured as MiG-21STMs but rebuilt to the MiG-21bis-standard before delivery to Iraq – were flown to Batajnica. One of these wore Iraqi serial number 21198 and was accepted for overhaul by Zmaj on 6 December 1989. Retaining its Iraqi serial, this jet was subsequently assigned to 126th Fighter Aviation Squadron and was flown against targets in eastern Slavonia during the late summer and autumn of 1991. During their overhaul, Iraqi MiGs received a camouflage pattern based on the one originally applied in the USSR but consisting of dark yellow sand (instead of beige) and the Yugoslav-made grey-green on upper surfaces and sides. (Artwork by Tom Cooper)

A pair of Mi-8 helicopters from 119th Aviation Brigade prior to the civil war in 1991, in which they played a large role in the transport of soldiers and medical evacuation. Blue-white Mi-8 helicopters were repainted, following the beginning of fighting, into standard olive-drab colour. (Mladen Savić)

The armed Yugoslav version of the Gazelle helicopter was designated Gama, and carried four Malyutka ATGMs, though they found few suitable targets in the civil war. A much more favourable solution for the nature of the clashes would have been the Mil Mi-24, which the RV i PVO tried to procure in the summer of 1991, but Moscow decided to decline. (Krila Armije)

Units flying the Jastreb light attack aircraft in the Yugoslav War in the summer of 1991 had significantly more assignments than those flying the heavier, faster, and more advanced Orao and G-4. (Media-centre Odbrana)

In March 1991 a pair of G-4 aircraft from 249th Fighter-Bomber Aviation Squadron was used for the conversion training of pilots from the Union of Myanmar, the first export customer for this type. Under the wings are practice concrete aerial bombs. Prior to the war in SFRJ, six G-4s were delivered to Myanmar. (Davor Lukić)

One of the most important offensive trump cards of the RV i PVO were British-made Hunting BL.755 CBUs, here seen carried by Orao serial number 25153 from 238th Fighter-Bomber Aviation Squadron. The aircraft in the photograph was used in battles in Slovenia and later in West Slavonia. It was destroyed in an accident in March 1992. (Mladen Savić)

MiG-21PFMs, acquired in 1967 and 1968, were the oldest aircraft of the RV i PVO in the civil war, but saw intensive deployment and flew dozens of CAS and BAI sorties. (Aleksandar Radić)

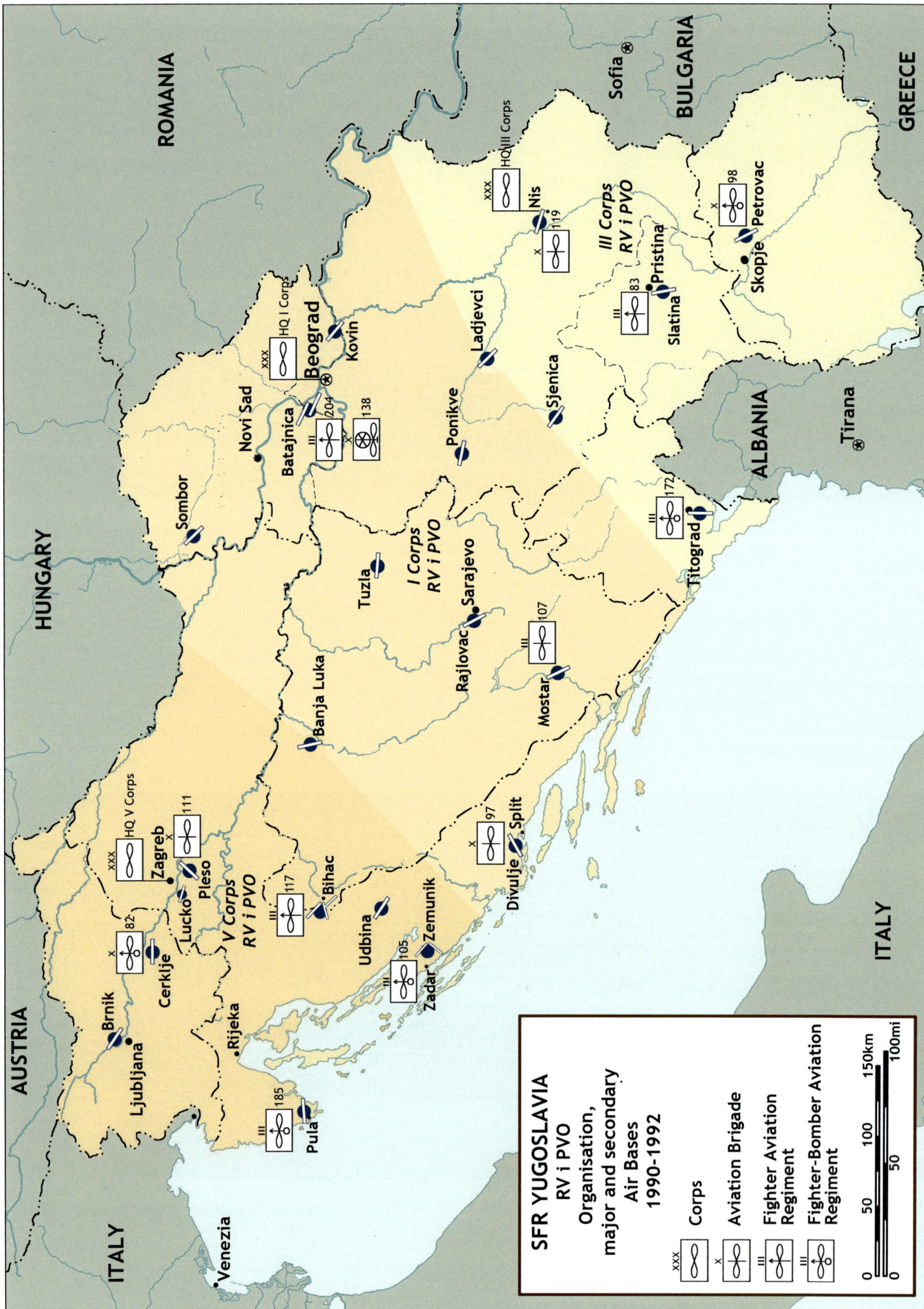

The SFRJ, with all the major air bases and secondary airfields used by the JRV i PVO as of 1990-1991. (Map by Tom Cooper)

Escape with a Gazelle

On 27 June, Gazelle helicopter serial number 12660, from Mrlak`s 2nd Flight of 894th RLAS, was relocated from Brnik to Maribor for use by the liaison Command of XXXI Corps. The crew, Captain 1st Class Jože Kalan and Sergeant Major Bogomir Šuštar, were flying visual reconnaissance. According to the recollection of Kalan, reported to journalists of the daily newspaper *Večer* in 1998, on the second day of the conflict, on 28 June, he found out from an officer sent from 111th Aviation Brigade at Pleso IAP, that an assault against their barracks was being prepared by a Mi-8 helicopter. He informed his colleague that it would be good to relocate the small Gazelle helicopter due to potential damage that could occur during the landing of a Mi-8 helicopter. He proposed to fly the Gazelle helicopter some 200m away from the pad it was on to the garage. He estimated that this was sufficient distance to reach speed and fly away in the direction of Austria, and he did that. He turned off the radio and took off towards Austria to create a false impression of where he was going and, after a minute – shortly before reaching the border – headed towards Pogorje. Kalan landed near the Golte hotel near Mozirje. He had not informed the TOS and units responsible for blocking a potential assault headed towards the landing site. Orders from the Command of 8th District HQ TOS, in Velenje, were not to shoot but to detain the crew. In the meantime, the hotel informed the Slovenes that the officers who had come with the Gazelle helicopter wanted to contact the command. Workers from the hotel and the TOS squad then helped apply provisional markings atop of those of the RV i PVO. Subsequently, Kalan and Šuštar were transferred to Mozirje where they were registered with the TOS and forwarded to a secret reception centre at a mountain lodge on Smrekovac, according to Plan Jezero for the reception of defectors from the JNA. The Gazelle helicopter was moved to a new secret location and remained in the hands of the TOS.[16]

Slovenian police hid away its air element in the forest, far from the main events. At that time, it had one AB.412, one AB.212, one A.109, and two AB.206B Jet Ranger III helicopters. (Emil Požar)

Gazelle serial 12660, whose crew defected from the RV i PVO, showing the provisional TO and Velenje markings of the new owner as applied in the field where it landed. (Tomaž Mrlak collection)

The Gazelle helicopter was camouflaged in the woods and remained in the hands of Slovenia. It was the only aircraft that remained from the RV i PVO in that newly formed state. (Tomaž Mrlak collection)

that were returning from the second wave. A shock, they shot down one and it crashed in flames…'

The commander of 82nd Aviation Brigade promptly called HQ V Corps JRV i PVO and demanded a suspension of heliborne transfers to border crossings. However, the officer in charge of the operation, Assistant Commander V Corps, Colonel Milan Maček reacted with an order for all the Mi-8s to fly at at least 300 metres altitude, in order not to upset the population. An angry Jerič concluded: 'It was like he fell from the Moon! (To their luck), the crews refused to listen to him!'[11]

Captain 1st Class Anton Mrlak (41) and his technician Sergeant Bojančo Stojanovski (32) were one of the three Gazelle-crews of 2nd Flight of 894th Squadron forward deployed at Šentvid since 25 June. Two days later, they were assigned to support the HQs of XIV and XXXI corps, JNA, in the Maribor area. They had already completed four sorties in the SA.341H serial number 12664, when they were ordered to pick up a load of bread from the JNA base in Kodeljevo and deliver it to Vrhnika. At 1919hrs, while underway at an altitude of only 100 metres over downtown Ljubljana, their Gazelle approached the part of the city with multiple government buildings. Of course, these were all well-protected, including two Strela-2M-teams of 30th Development Group positioned on nearby skyscrapers. Their first missile missed its target and hit the ground in the area of the Tivoli Park: ten seconds later, the second hit the helicopter, killing the crew. Both Slovenian teams were subsequently decorated for their feat.[12] The sad fate of Mrlak and Stojanovski was ironic: later on Kacin confirmed that Mrlak was one of three pilots of 894th Squadron's expecting to defect, flying his Gazelle to the Slovenian side at the first opportunity, however, once the fighting began, they lost contact with each other. Moreover, while both of the Slovenian Strela-2M-teams were decorated for their feat – which, obviously, was foremost undertaken for propaganda purposes – in 2000 the Slovenian authorities posthumously decorated Captain Mrlak as a Hero of Independence.[13]

Attack on Cerklje AB

Late in the evening of 27 June 1991, the commander of 238th Fighter Bomber Aviation Squadron, major Goran Bulut, scrambled from Cerklje AB in a single-seat IJ-21 to fly reconnaissance of the surrounding area. Although his aircraft was armed, Bulut received an explicit order from Jerič not to engage in any kind of combat. Shortly after getting airborne, the pilot sighted a column of 12 BOV-3 armoured vehicles of 580th Mixed Artillery Brigade, that was stopped by a barricade and surrounded by TOS troops while trying to reinforce defences of the biggest RV i PVO air base in Slovenia. Later on, this column attracted significant Slovenian attention, and suffered considerable losses in repeated attacks. Following Jerič's orders, Bulut returned and landed at Cerklje AB, but while doing so, saw several detonations to near the eastern end of the runway. Indeed, at 2045hrs, TOS attacked the base with ten 82mm mortar shells though the attack was then halted because the Slovenes expected a quick retaliation from several helicopters circling overhead.[14]

Although this attack caused no damage whatsoever, the RV i PVO was forced to conclude that its most important air base in Slovenia was in grave danger. Correspondingly, Jerič issued an order for locally based units to immediately start preparing for an evacuation. Under the cover of night, pilots of the Oraos from 238th Fighter Bomber Aviation Squadron, and 351st Reconnaissance Aviation Squadron flew their jets to Pleso IAP – only to find that the Croatian civilian authorities had switched off the runway lights. Nevertheless, the Oraos landed in the darkness.

Back at Cerklje AB, during the night of 27 to 28 June, a Croat paratrooper was killed under confusing circumstances in a friendly fire incident.[15]

First Combat Operations of the RV i PVO

As usual for this time of the year, the morning of 28 June 1991 was once again sunny and warm. The RV i PVO promptly exploited the opportunity to send multiple aircraft into reconnaissance over Slovenia. Simultaneously, it launched the transfer of remaining troops and Federal law-enforcement forces from Cerklje AB to the crucial Karawanks Tunnel. Once the reconnaissance aircraft returned and their photographs were developed it dawned upon the ŠVK that the Slovenes had erected a total of 15 massive roadblocks along the routes to the major border crossings, including not only those in Nova Gorica and the Karawanks, but also Šentilj, Murska Sobota, and Gornja Radgona. These blocked nearly all movement of the JNA's ground troops. Correspondingly, the ŠVK ordered nearly all of the fighter-bomber units deployed at Pula, Zemunik, and Bihać into action. The MiG-21s and G-4s of 185th Fighter Bomber Aviation Regiment, G-4s of 105th Fighter Bomber Aviation Regiment, and MiG-21s from 117th Fighter Aviation Regiment, were to operate either in pairs or in divisions of four aircraft.

That is when the next problem surfaced: two out of three squadron commanders and a large number of pilots of 82nd Aviation Brigade

In October 1988, during the demonstrations in Kosovo, transport missions were carried out using Yak-40 aircraft to move members of the SSUP. During the course of 1989 Yak-40 aircraft transported high-ranking officials of the Federation, Communist Party and the JNA from Belgrade to Priština. Prior to the armed conflict in Slovenia, on 25 June 1991, 675th TAS moved to elevated combat readiness. Yak-40s transported members of the SSUP and customs from Batajnica AB to Cerklje AB, from where Mi-8s flew them to border crossings. (Zdenko Molnar)

Mi-8 helicopter crews received infantry ballistic vests, manufactured at the Borovo factory, in a town of the same name, in East Slavonia. This example of a Mi-8 helicopter is serial 12239 from 780th THAS. (Tanjug)

Destroyed cars at Brnik IAP, after the actions of G-4 aircraft on 28 June. In the background are aircraft from the history of the RV i PVO, which were displayed on the airport – an F-84G Thunderjet, two F-86D Sabre Dogs, and a 522 piston trainer. (Borba)

openly refused to obey their orders. Indeed, turmoil subsequently spread at the base, as many of the personnel decided to leave, leaving the paratroopers of 63rd Brigade alone in the northern sector of the perimeter. Lieutenant-Colonel Jerič then asked one of his NCOs – who was a radio amateur – to establish contact with the TOS in the nearby town of Brežice and reached an agreement for a local ceasefire.

Oblivious of what was going on in Slovenia, other pilots of the RV i PVO went into action. Two from 237th Fighter Bomber Aviation Squadron – which operated a total of 13 J-21s and two NJ-21s – attacked the roadblock outside Trebnje, before landing at Zemunik AB in Dalmatia. Four Oraos removed from Cerklje AB the previous night, flew their attack from Pleso IAP, before landing at Bihać on their return (by then, all the other aircraft of 238th and 351st Squadrons had also transferred to Bihać AB).

G-4s from Pula hit several targets and flew in a demonstration of force over Brnik, They then went on to strike aircraft on the civilian side of the airport there, because the TOS and the Slovenian police were about to attack this installation. Flight activities there had been suspended since 1330hrs on 26 June by order of the Federal ATC. Aircraft belonging to Slovenian airline Adria Airways – an Airbus A320, one Douglas DC-9, and two de Havilland Canada Dash-7 aircraft – were all parked inside or around the same hangar. At 1015hrs on 18 June, a single G-4 strafed this hangar and a container used by the police with its GSh-23LY gun, and then with 57mm unguided rockets: these set on fire several airport vehicles and private cars. Moreover, the A320 (registration YU-AOE) was hit by both 23mm rounds and concrete debris that pierced the fuselage, fin, right horizontal rudder, and both engines; one Dash-7 (YU-AIF) received damage on its fuselage and the electric system, another (YU-AIE) had its wings, fuselage, and engine gondolas pierced; while the DC-9 escaped with 'only' a few holes.[17]

Immediately afterwards, high-ranking Slovenian officers joined the local TO unit, hoping to see a successful downing of the next G-4. However, they were disappointed: one Super Galeb never descended within the range of the MANPADS, and then a Strela-2M was fired at the other, but failed, and hit a nearby house instead. Finally, a second missile was fired at Mi-8 helicopters but went past its target without tracking. Tensions were also high outside the airport, and the crew of a JNA M-84 MBT shot up a car carrying two Austrian journalists with machine gun fire, suspecting them of being Slovenes that were carrying Armbrusts. In return, a Slovene sneaked up on the Federal tanks in the evening and fired a single anti-tank rocket: this wounded the commander of I Battalion of 1st Armoured Brigade, but in return the Slovene was killed by small arms fire.

Elsewhere, combat aircraft of the RV i PVO attempted to provide support for JNA units blocked in front of various barricades. At 0915hrs, the TOS attacked a column of BOV-3s that had come from Karlovac in the Medvedjek Gorge, and the officer in command promptly requested CAS. The air force responded with its first air strike at 1047hrs, then two more at 1130hrs, and the fourth at 1456hrs. These attacks were not particularly precise but saw the deployment of Hunting BL.755 CBUs that still seriously wounded five of the TOS, one of whom subsequently died. Much worse was the fate of six drivers of the trucks used in the roadblock: all were killed, together with one Slovenian civilian. The JNA lost two killed and two wounded in this clash. One G-4 – serial number 23636 – then collided with a bird on the way back to Pula, which caused its engine to surge: nevertheless, the pilot managed to nurse his aircraft back to base and make a successful emergency landing.

The Slovenian TO was very close to the airport. As there were houses between the auxiliary (in the foreground) and the main (visible in the background) runway, it is clear that in an open and longer conflict, defending the perimeter of the airport would be an extremely difficult task. The photo was taken in early July 1991 from a Mi-8 with attached pylons for UB-16-57 unguided rocket pods. (Mladen Savić)

In the Dravograd area, two MiG-21s made low-altitude, high-speed passes to intimidate a TOS unit that had blocked the approach to the southern entrance of the Karawanks Tunnel. The TOS opened fire at them from the nearby civilian airfield with four M55 guns, but all 22 shells fired missed their mark.[18] In the Kum area, the RV i PVO hit a tower with TV and radio repeaters, and wounded eight members of a TOS platoon deployed for its protection.

Much more attention followed the appearance of a single MiG-29 over Slovenia: the aircraft was underway on a combat air patrol (CAP) and, after concluding he had too little fuel to return all the way to Bihać AB, the pilot made a landing at Cerklje AB. At almost the same time a Mi-8 helicopter arrived to evacuate the body of a paratrooper from 63rd Brigade and it landed unmolested according to the agreement with the TOS. An honorary gun salute by paratroopers was also announced – in order to avoid disturbing the local population. Meanwhile refuelled, the MiG-29 then made a particularly noisy departure as the pilot pulled abruptly up and went into a vertical climb in full afterburner, in order to take his aircraft outside the range of the Slovenian MANPADS.

Overall, the fighter-bombers of the RV i PVO actually flew very little on 28 June as the ŠVK insisted on using combat aviation only in case of emergency, and then in the form of on-call missions on behalf of the JNA's units. With the HQ of 5th MD remaining reluctant in forwarding requests for CAS, the air force launched only between eight and 10 percent of the sorties it could have flown that day.

First Ceasefire

Deeply shocked by what had happened on the ground in Slovenia on 27 and 28 June, the SSNO and the ŠVK rushed to agree a truce with the Slovenian government, starting at 2100hrs on 28 June. However, the Slovenes had no motive to stop and during the night the fighting continued: indeed, the decision of the ŠVK to deploy only locally based units was indicative that it never planned to escalate the crisis into an all-out armed conflict. The Command of the RV i PVO was the only unit to think differently and on 28 June, it issued an order for the re-deployment of units from eastern Yugoslavia to bases in central Yugoslavia. Correspondingly, a day later, three G-4s and eight J-21s from Batajnica's 252nd Fighter Bomber Aviation Squadron were transferred to Banja Luka, and one flight of five IJ-21s from 354th Reconnaissance Aviation Squadron were transferred from Lađevci AB to Bihać AB. In turn, on 29 and 30 June, two An-26s were transferred from Pleso AB to Bihać AB. The commander of this flight, Major Vladimir Rajtar, and several other pilots of Croat nationality, were 'waiting for some kind of signal from the Croat authorities' and one of his pilots, Major Zdravko Kovačević, was even in touch with the chief of the Croat secret service, and constantly informed him of the situation at Pleso. However, nothing happened.[19]

On 30 June, the last three J-22s, two J-21s, and six IJ-21s still at Cerklje AB, were all flown out to Zemunik AB. For security reasons, none of the pilots was briefed about the destination of their flight, the transfer was undertaken in total radio silence, and under cover of jets from 252nd Fighter-Bomber Aviation Squadron. Because three G-2s and a J-21 lost radio connection and then contact to the rest of the formation during the flight, their pilots flew to Banja Luka. At Zemunik, a total of 30 aircraft – including three Oraos and 27 Galebs and Jastrebs – were ad-hoc formed into 82nd Aviation Brigade, armed with unguided rockets, and put on alert.

On 29 and 30 June, Mi-8s and Gazelles ran supply missions to different surrounded, blocked and advanced task forces around Slovenia. For example, at Gornja Radgona, elements of 32nd Mechanised Brigade – that almost reached the border crossing – were supplied with two military rations per soldier, 80kg of bread, some cooked food, water, ammunition, and uniforms. Although both sides had meanwhile accepted the ceasefire, this was frequently violated. Around 1700hrs on 1 July, a single Mi-8 carrying a load of bread for troops in the barracks of Slovenska Bistrica was fired upon by multiple assault rifles. The helicopter landed but was then not granted permission for take-off: indeed, once darkness fell, the Slovenes installed a spotlight at the nearby church, which illuminated its landing spot and a large part of the barracks. The helicopter was to remain there until 29 July 1991.

The situation was also tense in the area of two major RV i PVO radar stations in Slovenia; Ljubljanski Vrh occupied by I Company 51st Air Surveillance Battalion and equipped with a Marconi S-654 radar; and Oljska Gora occupied by III Company 51st Battalion, equipped with a Marconi S-600 and a Soviet-made P-15. Both were surrounded at the start of the conflict. On 1 July, two officers who had deserted from the unit on Oljska Gora called on the commander of the radar position to surrender. He refused the call and threatened to call air support, which was already airborne. He requested that the TOS move away from the zone of one kilometre around the perimeter. Units of the TO responded by mortaring the station at Ljubljanski Vrh. According to the recollection of the crew of the radar, during the night from 1 to 2 July, the TOS tried to take over the radar site and the crew fired back with assault rifles before receiving CAS from a single

Oraos Strafing

Perhaps the best example of the atmosphere during the first and second days of the War in Slovenia was the situation surrounding the famous border crossing at Šentilj/Spielfeld, on the highway connecting Maribor with Graz in Austria. At 0900hrs on 27 June, a column of 10 T-55 MBTs led by a BTR-50 command APC from the 31st Mechanised Brigade JNA, exited the barracks in Maribor and drove down the road for the border. They broke through one roadblock but then got struck at the second in the village of Pesinca. Although deploying their 100mm cannons to destroy the trucks blocking their way, the tanks failed to punch through and in the evening came under attack by a TOS team using 9K111 Fagot (ASCC/NATO-codename 'AT-4 Spigot') anti-tank guided missiles, which was beaten back by machine-gun fire, without losses for either side. Meanwhile, elements of 66th Border Guard Battalion from the posts in Šentilj and Ceršak surrounded the Slovene crew at the border crossing. Finally, around 1900hrs, four Mi-8 helicopters appeared to disembark 50 Federal Police and Customs officers near the Ceršak border post.

Early the next morning, 31st Mechanised Brigade re-launched its drive, and broke through only to run into another roadblock in the village of Štrihovec which consisted of no less than thirty 30-tonne tilt-trailed trucks and 20 railroad cars. As the tanks approached, an ambush was sprung and one of the T-55s was hit by an Armbrust and the crew of four – two of whom were wounded – jumped out and surrendered to the TOS. When the rest of the column attempted to pass through the yards of nearby houses, two tanks became bogged down. A mere kilometre short of the Šentilj border crossing, the remaining five T-55s ran into another roadblock.

Meanwhile, the commander of 31st Brigade requested air support, and the RV i PVO flew two attacks on the roadblock in Štrihovec at 1145hrs, without any effect. The second strike at 1330hrs set several trucks ablaze and also hit the police station at the border crossing. Tragically, four foreign truck-drivers were killed, including three Turks and one Bulgarian, while three Slovenian soldiers were wounded. In the course of these air strikes Yugoslav combat aircraft violated Austrian airspace several times, prompting the scramble of SAAB 35Ö Draken interceptors of the Austrian Air Force forward deployed at Graz/Thalerhof airport. Moreover, a RV i PVO MiG-21R flew reconnaissance all the way to the second-largest city of Austria, without being intercepted by the Austrians.

Nevertheless, by the morning of 29 June 1991, the condition of the detachment from 31st Mechanised Brigade was hopeless, as its tanks ran out of fuel and were short on ammunition. Recognising this fact, the commander of the column agreed to surrender: the TOS thus acquired its first six intact T-55s, which were promptly pressed into service with its first tank unit. Surely enough, the Federal officers had meanwhile secured the Šentilj border crossing, but on 2 July 1991 the TOS launched an attempt to recover this. While this assault was repulsed, the Federals lost their spirit and during the evening the JNA troops retreated towards the Ceršak post, or fled into the woods, 10 officers and other ranks crossed to the Austrian side and surrendered there, while the rest surrendered. The end of this drama came when the Border Guards also surrendered the nearby Ceršak post.

The post-scriptum followed in 1998, when the Slovenian police arrested Vladimir Bodiš, a former officer of the RV i PVO. Together with another former pilot of the JRV i PVO, Marjan Lovrić, the court in Maribor accused him of releasing 'prohibited ordnance,' in the form of BL.755 CBUs, at the roadblocks. The verdict was acquittal for lack of evidence: certainly enough, both Bodiš and Lovrić were former Orao-pilots of 238th Fighter Bomber Squadron, and both were ordered to attack the roadblock in Štrihovec on 29 June – but they both refused to follow their orders. Both had meanwhile joined the Croat air force and, tragically, then shared their ultimate fate: on 16 June 2011, they were both killed in an accident involving a Rans S-9 ultra-light aircraft.

MiG-21, which deployed SAB-100MN flare bombs, and then a pair of G-4s from Pula. Guided by the local radar controllers, they delivered precise attacks, prompting the Slovenes to give up and withdraw. For the following few nights, they only occasionally harassed the two stations with small-arms fire.[20] The Slovenes subsequently reported only the deployment of a 'powerful illuminating rocket' that night.

Demanding Retaliation

At the critical moments of the conflict in Slovenia, there was a strong current within the top ranks of the JNA to move decisively, hit the Slovenes with mass air strikes and then deploy reinforcements for ground forces. On 29 June, Chief of General Staff JNA, Colonel-General Blagoje Adžić, and 36 high-ranking officers arrived in Zagreb for a conference with the senior officers of 5th MD, including its commander, Colonel-General Konrad Kolšek, commander of V Corps RV i PVO, Major-General Rožić, and the Chief of Staff V Corps RV i PVO, Colonel Ljubomir Bajić. Adžić demanded severe retaliation against Slovenia and announced that three strikes against vital infrastructure of Slovenia, utilising every available aircraft of the air force, would be planned for the next day. Simultaneously, a mobilisation of all ground units of 1st and 3rd MD was initiated. However, not only was Kolšek openly opposing such ideas, but this plan was declined by General Kadijević. Instead, the air force was only granted permission to fly CAS on-call for threatened units. Nevertheless, subordinate officers began exercising pressure even after the decision had been taken. Early on the morning of 30 June, Kolšek

Ljubomir Bajić, Chief of Staff and then the commander of V Corps RV i PVO. The photograph was taken in the autumn of 1991 in Bihać near the MiG-21bis he used to fly. (Petar Bošković)

received a call from Bajić, who offered 'Comrade General, everything is ready, waiting for you to approve.'

Kolšek's response was a determined 'NO!', and he repeated his insistence on granting permission only for on-call sorties, and against selected targets. Still, even during a meeting of all top commanders of 5th MD on 1 July, many continued demanding a 'massive air strike on Ljubljana'. Meanwhile furious, Kolšek snapped back:

> You have aviation and artillery and can demolish whatever you want, but then you also have to carry the responsibility on your own! Provide military targeting information, and no civilian targeting information, and then request my decision!

Apparently, this was the drop that over spilled the barrel. At 1430hrs on 1 July, Kolšek was ordered to an urgent meeting with the ŠVK in Belgrade. The following night, the SSNO announced the assignment of a new commander of 5th MD in Zagreb, based on a decree signed on 29 June – supposedly kept confidential until that moment in time.[21] Appointed in Kolšek's place were two Serbs; Colonel General Života Avramović took over as the commander of 5th MD; while Colonel Bajić – a former MiG-21 pilot, and then the only one who ever made an emergency landing with a MiG-21 and survived – who had a reputation of being a 'sensible fighter pilot' and was 'expected to act decisively', was advanced in rank to Major-General and appointed as the new commander of V Corps RV i PVO.

Renewed Fighting

It was under these conditions that combat operations were resumed on 2 July 1991 by the TOS. Encouraged by the results of the first two days of the war, the Slovenes decided to finish the JNA in their republic. Certainly enough, Avramović promptly reacted by ordering the air force into action. However – and as so often in similar situations in many other conflicts around the globe – even his list of targets included 'only' roadblocks, TV-transmitters in Boč, Krvavec, Kum, and Nanos, and radio transmitters in Domžale, Ljubljanski Grad, and Trdinov Vrh. The latter were considered to be 'used to spread propaganda against federal authorities.' Obviously, regardless of how much 'decisive action' the generals of the JNA had demanded, and despite Kolšek's removal, nobody was ready to take the responsibility for causing widespread destruction and the death of civilians in Slovenia.

The hectic war atmosphere at Cerklje AB in July 1991 – pilots and technician-flyers in blue suits commence on their assignments. In the foreground is Gazelle serial 12893 that arrived from Batajnica AB and on the left side is a Gama with covered Malyutka ATGMs. (Mladen Savić)

The action in Slovenia on 2 July primarily revolved around multiple columns of JNA troops blocked during their advance towards border crossings or attempts to reinforce exposed air bases on 27 and 28 June. For example, a company of eight M-60 APCs of 4th Armoured Brigade received the order to secure several locations outside the towns of Brežice and Bregana, and the nearby Cerklje AB. While approaching this area, the column ran into a roadblock set up next to the village of Čatež

A flight of Mi-8s from Niš's 787th THS on Cerklje AB in July 1991. (Mladen Savić)

on the Sava River, and remained there for the next six days. Eventually, the commander of 4th Brigade deployed a battalion-sized task force to free the column, and then protect the Neva-M SAM-site defending Cerklje AB. Early on 2 July 1991, the relief column reached the blocked APC company, and then attempted to destroy the roadblock. Shortly after its tanks opened fire, at 0930hrs, they came under attack from the TOS. The commander requested CAS, while his M-84s attempted to drive around the obstacle. At around 1000hrs a single Jastreb of 252nd Fighter Bomber Aviation Squadron appeared overhead, dived and unleashed 5-inch HVAR unguided rockets upon the roadblock. Meanwhile, the Slovenes hit an M-84, causing it to blow up, de-facto stopping the advance. A new attempt was launched in the afternoon and at 1500hrs three Jastrebs attacked the roadblock and also, mistakenly, some of 4th Brigade's troops. Finally, in repeated counterattacks by the TOS, the column suffered the loss of two M-60s, and had three tanks and four APCs damaged, while losing one officer and two soldiers killed. Ultimately, the unit was withdrawn without reaching Cerklje AB.

The situation was similar in several other parts of Slovenia. A column of 12 BOV-3s blocked near Medvjedek since 28 June, attempted to break out, but was stopped by another roadblock outside Krakovski Gozd early on 2 July, and then attacked by the TOS at 0516hrs. The JNA commander promptly requested CAS and his message was obviously intercepted by the Slovenes, who quickly withdrew as when the jets appeared at 0643hrs, they fired their unguided rockets into abandoned positions of the TOS.

After the first actions on 27 June, Mi-8 helicopters that supplied isolated barracks and transported wounded soldiers were given provisional Red Cross markings, as on serial 12222 from 780th TAS filmed at its home base of Pleso. (Radoljub Matović)

In the summer of 1991 the key people in the hierarchy of the RV i PVO were commander of the service Lieutenant-General Zvonko Jurjević, middle, and commander of V Corps RV i PVO Colonel Ljubomir Bajić, closest to the camera. Note – Bajić has an official coat of arms of the SFRJ on his sleeve as a symbolic political message. On the left, in a blue pilot`s suit, is Major Ivan Baralić, commander of 238th Squadron. Lieutenant-General Nikola Uzelac, commander of V Corps JNA can be seen behind in a camouflage uniform and field cap. (Mladen Savić)

In the Ljubljana area, and in support of 1st Armoured Brigade, around 1545hrs two MiG-21UMs blasted the roadblock outside Vrhnika with 57mm unguided rockets. The TOS fired at least one Strela-2M in return, but this missed. Finally, four Jastrebs sent to fly power demonstration over Dravograd only served to provide training for the TOS gunners: the latter fired 150 rounds of 20mm, forcing all four pilots into a vertical climb out of range.

The Slovenes continued their attacks throughout 3 July, and thus the JRV i PVO flew additional air strikes, however – and despite SSNO's decision to 'carry out energetic air strikes on armed forces and some facilities in Slovenia' – these left no lasting impressions upon anybody. On the contrary, the mass of the air force did not take part in any action. Indeed, 82nd Aviation Brigade was re-deployed further away from the battlefield: two of its J-22s, one NJ-22 two-seater, four IJ-21s, and one G-2 were evacuated from Zemunik to Bihać, where they joined 238th Fighter Bomber Aviation Squadron and 351st Reconnaissance Aviation Squadron. During the evening 34 J-21s and G-2s were also transferred to Mostar.

Pilots from 237th Squadron at Udbina AB on 16 July 1991. The Jastreb aircraft behind has a SAB-100MN flare bomb under its wing. The pilot in the middle, with moustache and sunglasses, is Lieutenant Colonel Ljubomir Mraz who after the departure from 82nd Brigade in Cerklje, remained acting commander of the unit. (Mladen Savić)

Plan Grom and Political Settlement

According to the memoirs of General Kadijević – at the suggestion of the ŠVK and the Presidency of the SFRJ (without representatives of Croatia and Slovenia) – spent the day considering three military options:

1) To defeat the Slovenian armed forces and then leave the republic, nevertheless. For this option, the JNA was to reinforce its locally based units through the addition of three brigades and much stronger assets of the RV i PVO, and the operation was expected to last three days.
2) To force the leadership in Ljubljana to respect Federal authorities through an all-out application of air power, without reinforcing the JNA's ground units already present in Slovenia. However, because the ŠVK expected that the Slovenes would launch an insurgency in reaction, it was also forced to the conclusion that the air force would be unlikely to find cost-effective targets. Therefore, such an effort would require targeting the Slovenian infrastructure indirectly serving the war effort – such as telecommunication centres and factories manufacturing armament.
3) The final option was to achieve political goals through a combined operation of the Federal political leadership, and a limited operation of the JNA, always depending on the conduct of the Slovenes.

Kadijević claims that the SIV initially accepted the first option, while completely excluding the second, but that eventually 'some members' of the Presidency of the SFRJ refused to accept the first option completely. Ultimately, the most realistic – third – option was selected, and this could have ended only in one conclusion: a withdrawal from Slovenia.[22]

However, while the related meetings in Belgrade were still going on, late on 2 July, the plan for a large-scale air strike on Slovenia – Operation Grom – was finally completed by top commanders of the RV i PVO, and couriers began distributing it to the units. Dragoslav Spasojević, who served at Batajnica AB at the time, was hardly back home from a long day of work when, at 2200hrs, he received a telephone call to urgently report to HQ I Corps. Once there, he received an order to transfer the plan to Banja Luka AB, which he did by flying a G-2, half an hour after midnight. In reaction to this order, 252nd Fighter Bomber Aviation Squadron then prepared 14 of its aircraft for combat. At 0900hrs, these were spooling up their engines, when a new order arrived postponing take off until 1000hrs. A few hours later, the unit received the information that Operation Grom was suspended because a political solution had been reached.[23]

Indeed, contrary to the wishes of the senior officers of the JNA, the dynamics of the conflict were greatly reduced on 3 July, and a cease-fire agreed for the same evening. Under the same agreement, all the JNA units were to withdraw to their barracks. Thus, the only combat-like action of the day was that by Mi-8 serial number 12219 from 780th Squadron, which made an emergency landing in the village of Hrastje-Mota, near Gornja Radgona and in an attempt to avoid possible ground fire the pilot flew so low that he hit the trees below. Eventually, this helicopter became a spoil of war and was captured by the TOS and received corresponding – provisional – markings on the fuselage. Following necessary repairs, on 18 July it was flown to the airfield of the Rakičan aero-club, in Murska Sobota. A few days later, it was handed back to the RV i PVO.

Because it was still uncertain whether the fighting would resume or end, the RV i PVO meanwhile continued deploying reinforcements closer to Slovenia. On 7 July, 16 J-22 and 15 G-4s with 60 pilots, 109 officers and NCOs, and 82 soldiers of 172nd Fighter-Bomber Aviation Regiment from Golubovci AB, were transferred to Tuzla AB, while units based at Pula, Zemunik, Bihać, and Banja Luka were kept on almost permanent combat alert. On the contrary, the remnants of 82nd Aviation Brigade continued switching bases: on 9 July 1991, J-21s and G-2s from 237th Fighter-Bomber Aviation Squadron transferred from Mostar AB to Udbina AB, inside the SAO Krajina, which until then served as a dispersal site for Bihać AB and had no permanently assigned units. 238th Fighter-Bomber Aviation Squadron and 351st Reconnaissance Aviation Squadron remained at Bihać.

That said, the war in Slovenia ended on 7 July when, under the mediation of the European Community (EC; subsequently the European Union), the Brioni Declaration was signed by both of the involved parties. Under this agreement, all combat operations were to immediately case, the EC deployed its Monitor Mission (ECMM), and a three-month moratorium on the implementation of the declaration of independence of Croatia and Slovenia was announced, pending the withdrawal of all JNA assets from Slovenia. For all practical purposes, the Bironi Declaration meant an end of the SFRJ as it used to be, a withdrawal of Federal forces and the independence of Slovenia.

Of course, tensions remained high for a while longer and, time and again, the air force was called to help resolve crises with power demonstrations. On 12 July 1991, the commander of 5th Aerial Surveillance Regiment was about to tour the radar stations under his command in a Gazelle helicopter, when the TOS banned the take-off. Eventually, the new commander of V Corps RV i PVO, Colonel Bajić, ordered two MiG-21bis from Bihać and two G-4s from Pula to provide top cover, and the officer was able to complete his inspection. Finally, on 17 July, two Oraos from 242nd Fighter-Bomber Aviation

Squadron carried out four sorties at extremely low altitude along the route from Cerklje via Kranj to Kočevje, demonstrating the power and resolve of the Federal forces to use it. Similar missions were carried out by other squadrons during the following days.

Withdrawal from Slovenia

On 18 July 1991, the last President of the SIV, Stipe Mesić, signed the decision for the general withdrawal of Federal armed forces from Slovenia. The order was confirmed by the SSNO and the ŠVK on 25 July, and a decision was taken to carry it out between 27 July and 18 October. Throughout this period, the RV i PVO was to continue flying reconnaissance and airspace-control operations, to provide top cover for truck-convoys carrying JNA units eastwards, and to remain on alert for possible combat operations. During further negotiations, the Slovenian authorities attempted to force the Federals to leave behind their entire aerial surveillance network and the Neva-M SAM-site protecting Cerklje, but the JNA refused. Nevertheless, the Federals were forced to leave up to 70 percent of the heavy equipment – including Gazelle serial number 12660 – in Slovenia. Cerklje AB was left intact, but heavily mine-infested: reportedly, the TOS subsequently had to remove 209 anti-personnel mines, 30 anti-tank mines, and 63kg of TNT from the perimeter of the base, and 1,160kg of TNT from under the runway.

More important was the issue of military professionals of Slovenian nationality: these were given the option to continue serving with the JNA, or to quit military service. The, once powerful 82nd Aviation Brigade was to feel the rift along the ethnic lines most severely. Its commander, Lieutenant-Colonel Jerič, was granted early retirement and continued living in Brežice. However, both the commander of 351st Reconnaissance Aviation Squadron and his two assistants, and the commanders of its 1st and 2nd Flights deserted. Eventually, 77 officers and other ranks of this unit defected or requested permission to quit the service. Of only 12 pilots that continued serving and flying Oraos, eight were Slovenes, two Croats, one Yugoslav, and one Serb. Another unit to feel the split strongly was 105th Fighter-Bomber Regiment, where 18 pilots decided to leave, and their total number thus decreased from 102 to 84. Similarly, out of 28 pilots assigned to 679th Transport Aviation Squadron, 18 left to join the ZNG.[24]

A view from entrance No. 2 to the underground galleries of Objekt Klek at Bihać AB, at the beginning of July 1991. On the left side of the frame is a MiG-21bis prepared for a mission with four 57 mm unguided rocket pods. (Mladen Savić)

Flag platoon at the formation ceremony of 238th Squadron in Banja Luka AB on 11 August 1991. The RV i PVO entered the civil war in characteristic blue pilot suits, technicians in dark blue work uniforms, and soldiers in M77 uniforms that had characteristic light blue shirts that were visible at a great distance. (Mladen Savić)

Pilots of 238th Squadron stand in front of Orao aircraft serial 25119. All are armed with standard 7.65mm Zastava M70 service pistols, in accordance with war-time regulations. (Mladen Savić)

While the withdrawal was initially mostly by road, due to the subsequent outbreak of war in Croatia during the summer of 1991, the withdrawal was largely undertaken by the sea from the port of

Koper. Because of this, it took a week longer than originally planned, and was concluded only on 25 October.

Overall, during the short war in Slovenia, according to the official documentation the JRV i PVO suffered the loss of one Gazelle and one Mi-8 shot down; one Gazelle flown away by a defecting pilot, while several other aircraft and helicopters suffered various degrees of damage by small-arms fire. Other than two Slovenian MANPADS known to have scored direct hits, all others had missed their mark. Out of 37 members of the JNA killed during the conflict, six were from the RV i PVO: five crewmembers of the downed helicopters, and one paratrooper.

Disestablishment of 82nd Brigade

The withdrawal from Slovenia prompted the RV i PVO into a reorganisation of multiple units and further transfers and exchanges of aircraft. Units originally based at Cerklje AB, and temporarily based at Zemunik, Bihać, and Udbine, eventually found a new home at Banja Luka AB. Operated by the personnel of 474th Air Base, this airfield constructed in 1982 had a 1,860m long runway, eight HAS and two hardened shelters for command and control facilities, and was used as a forward operating base (FOB) by 252nd Fighter-Bomber Aviation Squadron during the summer of 1991. Oraos from Bihać and Jastrebs from Udbine were transferred to Banja Luka AB on 11 August 1991.

However, as soon as 82nd Aviation Brigade completed its transfer to its new home-base, this unit and all its elements were disbanded. 351st Reconnaissance Aviation Squadron was deleted from the list of the RV i PVO's units, and its aircraft (including IJ-21s 24406, 24407, 24421, 24423, 24425 and 24456, and G-2s 23133 and 23178) transferred to 352nd Reconnaissance Aircraft Squadron at Bihać AB. The IJ-21s with serial numbers 24410 and 24429, were re-assigned to 252nd Fighter-Bomber Aviation Squadron, and G-2s 23158 and 23212 to 240th Fighter-Bomber Aviation Squadron. Similarly, its Jastrebs were handed over to other units: five (24133, 24136, 24139, 24208 and 24212) to 252nd Fighter-Bomber Aviation Squadron, three (2411, 24141, and 24275) to 240th Fighter-Bomber Aviation Squadron, while one (24158) was sent for repairs to the Zmaj Works. Galeb-2s 23181 and 23182 were handed over to 240th Squadron, and 23120 to 252nd Squadron.

Jastrebs of disbanded 237th Squadron and Oraos of former 238th Squadron were all integrated into the re-organised 238th Fighter-Bomber Aviation Squadron and then – following an order of the SSNO from 30 August 1991 – this unit was re-assigned to Bihać's 117th Fighter Aviation Regiment, which on the same date was re-organised into 117th Aviation Brigade.

View from a Gazelle helicopter of a column of vehicles, carrying parts of S-125M Neva-M SAMs from 350th Air Defence Missile Regiment, on the road from Slovenia to Belgrade. The first vehicle is a Kraz-214, which is towing a 5P73 launcher and it is followed by a PR-14 (based on a ZIL-131) that is carrying two 5V27 missiles. The Belgrade-based 250th Air Defence Missile Brigade was reinforced and increased the number of its battalions from four to eight with this equipment (Mladen Savić)

5V27 Missiles for S-125M Neva-M SAM-system as seen at Vrhnika base in early July 1991 when preparations for the relocation of 350th ADM Regiment started. (Mladen Savić)

A P-15 2D surveillance radar (NATO-code Flat Face) in a column of equipment that was being pulled out of Slovenia, via Croatia, in August 1991. (Mladen Savić)

Table 6: Aircraft of the reorganised 238th Fighter-Bomber Squadron, August 1991

Type	Serial Numbers
J-21	24148, 24160, 24202, 24205, 24209, 24218, 24251, 24258
J-22	25106, 25111, 25114, 25115, 25116, 25119, 25122, 25123, 25153
INJ-22	25503, 25504
NJ-22	23509, 23511
V-51	51127

Reorganisation of Aerial Surveillance and Air Defence Units

Having secured the retention of all of its early warning radars based in Slovenia, the RV i PVO subsequently took care to re-distribute these as follows:

- Radars from Ljubljanski Vrh were re-located to Plješevica Mountain, above Bihać AB
- Radars from Oljska Gora to Titograd in Montenegro

350th Air Defence Missile Regiment, which used to consist of four battalions of Neva-M SAMs and one technical support battalion, was originally planned to be re-located to Mostar. However, since it took time to construct its new positions, only two battalions were transferred there, while the other two travelled along the highway connecting Zagreb with Belgrade to Obrenovac and Jakovo in Serbia.

More problematic was the personnel situation of this unit, as only 51 officers and 75 other ranks remained with it (of these, 68 were Serbs, 20 Yugoslavs, 12 Macedonians, 9 Muslims, 6 Croats, 4 Montenegrins, 3 Hungarians, 2 Albanians, 1 Czech, and 1 Ruthenian).

4 CRISIS IN CROATIA

Once the future of Slovenia was decided, a big question mark hung over the future of Croatia. The government and its supporters in Zagreb were split: hardliners demanded not only harsh action against Croatian Serbs and attacks on the JNA, but also securing large parts of Bosnia and Herzegovina; knowing his forces lacked both heavy weapons and experience, President Tuđman officially sought to achieve a peaceful separation of an intact Croatia from the SFRJ, while actually seeking ways to not only receive support of the international community, but indeed to attempt effecting a foreign military intervention. After successfully establishing itself in control of the SAO Krajina, the Serbian leadership in Croatia, supported by Serbia, designed a plan to expand its control over additional areas through apparently unplanned, undirected, and incoherent local attacks, which were to mask their actual intentions: a separation from Croatia, whether it seceded from the SFRJ or not. In Belgrade, Milošević and his supporters began propagating their vision of a rump Yugoslavia that included the Serb-controlled regions of Croatia, but without the rest of Croatia (and Slovenia). Firmly devoted to its ideal of protecting the SFRJ, the JNA tried hard to act as a peace-keeper, but failed: while the mass of its commanders still attempted to act neutrally, they gradually descended into support of Serb interests, thus confirming Croat suspicions. Initially, occasional public demonstrations in Croatia were thus followed by fire-fights in which inhabitants of one village would shoot at those of another, until the Federal armed forces moved in to separate them, only for another clash to erupt somewhere else. As the number of incidents increased, ever larger forces of the ZNG and the Serbian militias became involved: the security situation continuously degenerated and Croatia eventually found itself not only exposed to attacks from multiple directions, but in a strategic defensive.

Intimidation

Realising that several of its air bases were about to find themselves isolated deep within Croat territory, the air force rushed detachments of 63rd Parachute Brigade to Pleso, Pula, Bihać, and Zemunik. Flying units based there continued with their routine training in July and August and gradually this became ever more realistic, as the strict ban on flying below an altitude of 200 metres was lifted, and every pilot received the opportunity to hone his skills by flying simulated strikes on nearby ranges. MiG-21 and MiG-29 pilots from 204th FAR spent the summer of 1991 training at extremely low altitudes at the Čenta range in Banat, in north-western Serbia. MiG-21s from Bihać usually flew CAPs along a route connecting Pakrac with Bjelovar and Karlovac. Those of 252nd Fighter-Bomber Aviation Squadron flew dozens of training sorties from Kovin airfield (not used in peacetime), and some Galeb and Jastreb pilots even received additional conversion training for Kragujs evacuated from Slovenia. Reconnaissance units flew daily visual and photo-sorties, according to the assessment of the situation on the ground by the command of the RV i PVO and that of V Corps of the air force. A large number of reconnaissance sorties were coordinated with the movement of road convoys carrying units withdrawing from Slovenia.

The ŠVK regularly tasked units with flying shows of force at very low altitudes over various conflict zones. Such actions proved to be pointless and began drawing ever higher volumes of ground fire from Croat forces in July and August 1991. Nevertheless, they were continued, even if growing particularly risky whenever the pilots attempted to fly lower and make additional passes over targets in order to get a better look at the situation on the ground. Furthermore, MiG-21 pilots from Bihać AB were frequently tasked with low-altitude overflights of major Croat cities, usually at night between

After the end of the fighting in Slovenia, the situation on the ground was constantly monitored by flights of reconnaissance aircraft. Here there are three MiG-21R jets on duty at Bihać AB in mid-July 1991 – the first two with container D for daytime aerial photography, the third aircraft has container R for ELINT. The fourth was a two-seater MiG-21US trainer. (Mladen Savić)

The boarding of a task force of 63rd Parachute Brigade on an An-26, at Niš AB, for transport to Bihać AB. They were to secure that base and protect a wider area from potential attack by Croats from July 1991 to May 1992. (Boško Čeliković)

In the summer of 1992, the pilots of the Montenegrin TO squadron underwent training on J-20 Kragujs at Tivat airport, on the Adriatic Cost, located a couple of dozen kilometres of direct flight from Croatia. (Svetozar Jokanović collection)

0100hrs and 0300hrs, and with intercepts of commercial aircraft in all weather conditions. The lonesome MiG-21 unit based at Pula AB flew constant reconnaissance along the Adriatic coast, frequently reaching the limit of their tactical radius while checking vessels at sea. The reason was that the military intelligence services estimated that there was a high risk of infiltration of Croat volunteers and/or Western mercenaries from abroad or attempts to smuggle armament. Finally, frequent small-scale clashes between the ZNG and Serbian militias prompted the command of the RV i PVO into ordering regular CAPs by armed aircraft all over Croatia, because of the presumption that the psychological effects of such operations would be more effective than actual combat operations. Therefore, Dalmatia and Lika were covered by jets from 105th Fighter-Bomber Aviation Regiment and Kordun and Banija, and western and eastern Slavonia by 252nd Fighter-Bomber Squadron.

Summer over Slavonia

During June and July 1991, the Croat police and the National Guard began deploying a number of small, platoon-sized units in minor bases along the Danube River, on the border with Serbia. These were regularly overflown by the aircraft of the RV i PVO, although these frequently received ground fire. At first, pilots were prohibited from firing back, they were then granted permission to do so – provided they had carefully examined the position in question. Then the situation experienced a dramatic change.

On 8 July 1991, a column of JNA T-55s and 30mm M53/59 Praga self-propelled anti-aircraft guns crossed the Danube River bridge near the FOB of 1st Brigade ZNG in Principovac and surrounded the site. In the ensuing exchange of fire, a Praga destroyed a Croat police vehicle, while the Croats hit one of the MBTs with an RPG-7 rocket-propelled grenade. On 9 July 1991, the RV i PVO then received a direct order to destroy the FOB in Principovac. At 1600hrs, a single G-4 passed over, drawing anti-aircraft fire. Intending to hit back with 57mm unguided rockets, the pilot turned around, only to realise that his weapons would not fire. He quickly selected the GSh-23LY gun pod and delivered a very precise attack in which one ZNG solider was killed and two injured.

Four days later, another G-4 came under fire while underway over the area of Vukovar – a town in Croatia on the Danube River, which was in the process of being surrounded by JNA units – and retaliated with an attack on a Croat observation post atop a silo in the village of Bršadin.

On 13 July, Utva-75 serial number 53242 flown by Captain 1st Class Ivan Zabunov (with Lieutenant-Colonel Dušan Radaković) was hit by ground fire while underway from Udbine AB to Zemunik AB, while passing above the village of Karin. Feeling a burning sensation in his left shoulder, and then seeing a hole in the instrument panel, the pilot promptly descended from an altitude of 100 metres to 50 metres above ground and continued to Zemunik over the sea. Once on the ground, he and the ground crew realised that one bullet had penetrated the windshield and the instrument panel to scratch

A number of aircraft from 252nd Squadron were transferred from Batajnica AB to Kovin airfield in the region of Banat, for combat training courses. Aircraft took off from the runway, that had originally been built for the Luftwaffe during the Second World War, to practise shooting at the range at Čenta. This Galeb-2 is being prepared for a flight and is armed with 5-inch HVAR rockets. (672nd Automobile Training Centre)

In July 1992, pilots from 251st squadron at Kovin airfield underwent combat training on J-20 Kragujs. The aircraft were armed with 57mm unguided rocket launchers. (672nd Automobile Training Centre)

the cable of the headset worn by Radaković, while another pierced the left flap. Even more serious was the encounter a G-4-pilot from 252nd Fighter-Bomber Squadron had with a Croat-operated Strela-2M MANPAD while underway over the village of Mlaka in the Jasenovac area of the Posavina region, in central Croatia, on 16 July: he only managed to avoid the missile by flying a very hard turn. Less lucky was an IJ-21 Jastreb from 240th Fighter-Bomber Aviation Squadron in Mostar on 19 July which was hit by ground fire over the village of Bršadin but returned safely to Batajnica AB.

After the transfer from Pleso AB in July 1991, the helicopters were temporarily on runway Number 5 of Bihać AB. Visible in the background is one of the entrances into Objekt Klek's underground galleries in Plješevica Mountain where MiG-21s from 117th FAR were stationed. In the foreground is the Mi-8 serial 12366, which was temporarily added to 780th THS from 890th THS. (Mladen Savić)

Novi Čakovci Affair

On 22 July 1991 pilots of two Jastreb aircraft, serials 24116 and 24122, were on a visual reconnaissance of the situation in Mirkovci, in eastern Slavonia, where the ZNG was exercising pressure upon the Serbian

From 29 June to 11 August 1991, Banja Luka AB accommodated a detachment from 252nd Squadron with a mixed structure of Galeb-4s, Jastrebs, and Galeb-2s. (252nd Squadron)

The return of a Galeb-2 from 252nd Squadron from a mission to Banja Luka AB. In the summer of 1991, two-seaters were useful in visual reconnaissance missions while the limited combat load, usually reduced to a pair of 5-inch HVAR rockets and two 12.7mm machine guns, was sufficient for occasional action. (252nd Squadron)

In summer 1991, the morale in 252nd Squadron was exceptionally high and the unit showed great will to complete combat missions. Pilots flew in blue suits, but they repainted their helmets from white to camouflage tones in the same colours as their aircraft. (252nd Squadron)

Jastreb serial 24122 was damaged in an incident over Novi Čakovci on 22 July 1991. At the beginning of the civil war, aircraft damage from assault rifles was the subject of detailed military police investigation and the collection of evidence was part of the process of preparation for criminal proceedings for armed rebellion. Later, open war nullified any plans to investigate and prosecute Croatian soldiers who fired on aircraft. (Mladen Savić)

The characteristic combat load for Galeb-4s during flights in 1991 were two L-128-04 four-barrel launchers, two fuel tanks, and a pod for GSh-23LY 23mm guns. (Josip Novak)

TO. On reaching the village of Novi Čakovci, the pilots were surprised to detect a training centre for the local Croatian forces within a former primary school. At 1405hrs, both jets were hit by ground fire, but their pilots managed to return safely to Batajnica AB. Another pair – this time consisting of one IJ-21 Jastreb and one Galeb-2 – was sent to investigate. Upon reaching Novi Čakovci around 1705hrs, both aircraft received ground fire, but this time the pilots responded with machine gun fire and in the course of their strafing runs, two soldiers of 1st Brigade ZNG were killed and seven wounded, and a secondary explosion of ordnance was recorded.

The same evening, Serbian TV showed the damage to the aircraft hit by the Croat ground fire.[1] Indeed, the reaction of the upper echelons of the JNA to the incident at Novi Čakovci was 'determination': Lieutenant-General Jurjević ordered the pilots from 252nd Squadron to henceforth operate at altitudes of 500, 800 and more metres, reasoning that from those altitudes they could better see – while not being shot at. That said, the attitude of the RV i PVO command was confused, and the majority of generals preferred to ignore the reality of war. One example of this state of mind was the arrival of a team deputed by the High Command to 252nd Squadron on 23 July, with the task of investigating the option of using older Utva-66 liaison aircraft to deploy tear gas for 'riot control' in Croatia. Obviously, some were still thinking about the situation in terms of a 'police action'.

Atmosphere of Limited Engagement

For all practical purposes, the conclusion is unavoidable that as of July 1991 the SSNO, the ŠVK, and the commanders of the RV i PVO, could still not decide if they should engage in war or not. This became obvious when the Croats – the hardliners amongst whom saw the Federal armed forces as pro-Serb – began intercepting trains carrying the equipment of the JNA from Slovenia in an eastern direction and began unloading these as they wanted. Although the content of more than 50 railway cars was stolen just on the railway line from Zagreb to Slavonski Brod between 15 and 25 July, reconnaissance aircraft were sent to photograph emptied trains only – even once videos taken by cameras installed on several IJ-21 Jastrebs and Galeb-2s from the 252nd Fighter-Bomber Aviation Squadron had clearly shown Croatian troops fleeing from the scene when 'caught in the act'.

Instead, the same squadron was ordered to strike the ZNG's training centre in Erdut, on 25 July. This was a highly successful operation, that left five Croat troops dead and eleven wounded, and prompted the ZNG to withdraw from this base – which was subsequently taken by the paramilitary force of the notorious Serbian warlord Željko Ražnatović 'Arkan'.

However, perhaps the best example of the 'atmosphere of limited engagement' that dictated the pace of operations by the RV i PVO during this period occurred on 27 July 1991. When clashes between the ZNG and the Serb militias erupted in Kostajnica, in Central Croatia, the air force sent one of its jets into reconnaissance only. The sole strike missions flown had targeted – and destroyed – the small ZNG base in Opatovac, near Ilok, the easternmost town in Croatia. No casualties were reported but it is known that the local Croat unit was subsequently re-deployed to Vukovar. Things changed only very little, two days later, when members of 110th Brigade ZNG stopped a JNA column underway along the highway from Zagreb to Karlovac and disarmed the troops in the leading vehicle. For hours, there was no reaction from the ŠVK and it was only in the afternoon that HQ 5th MD ordered two armed MiG-21s to make a low-altitude pass. The column was then allowed to pass.

A similar situation on 30 July was sorted out at the discretion of pilots, not that of the generals. Two jets from 252nd Squadron flying escort for a column of trucks hauling equipment from Cerklje AB to Banja Luka received ground fire and their pilots came back to hit the offenders with volleys of 57mm S-5M unguided rockets. The target turned out the be the local school building, used by the Croatian police unit Roda, as confirmed by the fact that a police officer was killed. Similarly, when a pair of IJ-21s from the same unit was fired upon while overflying Kostajnica, their pilots returned fire with 57mm S-5Ms.

Second Wave of Defections

In June 1991, the Croat authorities impounded a Reims/Cessna F.172N and a Utva-75 of the Sinj aeroclub, and then pressed them to fly reconnaissance for the ZNG. By July, both aircraft received makeshift weapons and began flying air strikes against the SAO Krajina, too – all of which were officially declared as being 'tourist flights' and 'fire-fighting reconnaissance'. Neither the ŠVK nor the authorities of the SAO Krajina considered any such operations to be 'significant', however, once their frequency increased, the Federal authorities officially banned all flights from Sinj. Certainly enough, Serbian troops of the TO in the SAO Krajina were anything other than restrained and when facing one Croat air strike, they returned fire, forcing the Utva-75 pilot into violent evasive manoeuvring, in the course of which he hit a power line, badly damaging the wing of his aircraft.

More serious was the crisis that subsequently ocurred on Šolta – one of about 1,000 islands off the Croatian coast of the Adriatic Sea. On 5 August 1991, the Croats overran the local JNA outpost, capturing 6,000 rounds of 20mm ammunition. The JNA reacted by launching a heliborne counterattack – including a Mi-8 of 790th Transport Helicopter Squadron – and a naval blockade. The Croats were in urgent need of such ammunition because they had also captured four Oerlikon anti-aircraft guns from the TO on the island of Brač. The heliborne-intervention was in vain: the Croats managed to extract the ammunition and bring it to the mainland with help of one of the local ferries. Ultimately however, the Croats established that the ammunition they had seized could not be used on their Oerlikons, because it was for the 20mm Zastva-made AAG.. Finally boxes with

Iraqi Jets

The general withdrawal of the JNA and the RV i PVO put a giant question mark over one of the most important elements of technical support for the air force: the Zmaj Works in Velika Gorica, south-west of Zagreb, was one of two principal overhaul facilities in the SFRJ of the 1980s. It was officially certified to work on types such as the G-2, G-4, J-21, and MiG-21, and was in the process of being certified for the overhaul of MiG-29s. The quality of the work provided by Zmaj was high, and thus the company was repeatedly contracted to overhaul aircraft of foreign customers, including Egypt, Libya and Sudan, thus providing a valuable contribution to the depleted foreign exchange reserves of the SFRJ during the economic crisis of the 1980s. In 1988, shortly after the end of the Iran-Iraq War, its representatives were successful in securing a big order for the general overhaul of 20 MiG-21s and medium overhaul of 10 MiG-23s of the Iraq Air Force (IrAF). The IrAF was keen to renovate its resources because many of its aircraft were worn out by years of continuous warfare or had been damaged in combat. With overhaul facilities in the USSR already being overwhelmed with similar requests, and anxious to have its aircraft back as soon as possible, the Iraqis decided to have even their MiG-23s reworked by Zmaj. Because both the factory and the RV i PVO lacked the necessary technical documentation, these had to be obtained from Hungary, where the test pilot of the plant, Major Omer Avdaković also underwent a conversion course for MiG-23MF and MiG-23UB in autumn 1989. Meanwhile, Iraqi MiGs began arriving: one or two were usually delivered by Ilyushin Il-76 transports of the Iraqi Air Force, and the work on them commenced. The overhaul of MiG-21s proceeded quite straightforwardly, although it turned out that many were originally MiG-21SMTs, upgraded to the MiG-21bis standard (Izdeliye-50bis): Yugoslav documentation thus quoted them as MiG-21SMTs or, more frequently, as MiG-21IQs. The work on the first five was completed during the first half of 1990, and they were returned to Iraq within six months of arrival at Zmaj. Correspondingly, the Iraqis enthusiastically delivered additional MiGs. Work on the MiG-23s proceeded at a slower pace, and the Yugoslavs used one – serial number 23269 – for trials and testing their methods of overhaul. The work on this jet was completed in June, and it made its first test flight in July 1990.

The only intact Iraqi MiG-23ML extracted from the Zmaj Works – serial number 23269 – was on display at the Aeronautical Museim in Surčin, from 2000 to 2009. Following Iraqi requests for an overhaul and upgrade, it was subsequently transferred to Batajnica, where it is still stored. The assessment of the technical condition of the MiG-23ML radar was carried out by Lieutenant Colonel Aleksandar Kostić from the VTI, and he remembers that they had visible damage from the fighting. In the photo, Kostić is seen inspecting the MiG-23ML serial number 23252: this had bullet damage to its radar and its repairs and overhaul in the SFRJ were impossible. (Vojkan Kostić collection)

rounds were sent to Slavonia for the Croat units there, which had Zastava-guns.[2]

Hard on the heels of the first wave of defections during and immediately after the war in Slovenia, in the first half of August both the JNA and the RV i PVO began feeling ever wider disruptions caused by growing dissent from within, and then an ever larger number of defections of Croat officers. By far the most painful of these was when Colonel Imra Agotić, chief of security of V Corps RV i PVO, decided to quit his service. Officers like him were excellently informed about all details of the units in the field, their commanders and other ranks, and their equipment and bases. Moreover, Agotić and several other defectors were quick to join the ZNG and then to organise a system to monitor the activities of the air force with the help of telephones and radios. Finally, they organised a team based in Tuškanac (north-eastern suburb of Zagreb) for the reception of defecting members of the air force with the intention of retaining their know-how and setting up a Croat air force.

Finally, the crisis surrounding the JNA's units withdrawing from Slovenia and northern Croatia continued to escalate, as the ZNG continued interrupting the flow of their columns. On 11 August, the

Iraqi Jets (*continued*)

However, in August 1990, all further work was suspended when the United Nations (UN) imposed an arms embargo upon Iraq as a consequence of its aggression on Kuwait. By the time, most of the Iraqi MiGs still at Zmaj were in disassembled condition, and thus their parts were stored, pending a decision about their future.

Due to continuously increasing tensions in Croatia, the Command of the RV i PVO first improved the security of the plant through the deployment of a task force from 63rd Parachute Brigade. However, regular work was interrupted, and during the first week of July, the decision was taken to evacuate 12 MiG-21s in intact condition to Batajnica AB: some of these had been completely overhauled by this time, while the work on others had not commenced. Eight of these jets – including three former Iraqi jets – were eventually handed over to 126th Fighter Aviation Squadron. All retained their 'desert' camouflage scheme, which – consisting of sand and green – stood out from the light grey overall applied on all the MiG-21bis of the RV i PVO. Nevertheless, they retained their Iraqi five-digit serials 21168, 21198, and 21204, but their application in Persian digits was overpainted in green, and then they were re-applied in Arabic digits. As such, they were registered in the records of the air force, too.

Even then, there was still a question of what to do with the remaining aircraft and stockpiles of ordnance still at the Zmaj Works. As of mid-July, these included 15 MiG-21s, 10 MiG-23MLs, eight G-4s, nine G-2s, two J-21s, and a Pe-2FT twin-engined bomber left over from the 1940s, on revision for the Aeronautical Museum in Surčin. All of these in disassembled condition. Eventually, following additional negotiations with Zagreb – and despite much uproar in the Croatian media – Avdaković flew out MiG-23ML serial number 23269 to Batajnica AB, while all the other Iraqi MiGs were evacuated by road. While the ML ended at the museum in Surčin, the other aircraft were never re-assembled.

It was difficult to get a camera into the blocked garrisons, both as an unnecessary load and because the officers of the security service were very rigid and strictly forbade photography. Despite the photo bans however, some photographs were taken, such as the one in which a reservist from 63rd Parachute Brigade poses next to a MiG-23ML at Pleso AB. (Boško Čeliković collection)

Croats stopped a column approaching the bridge over the Sava River near Bosanska Gradiška, and it took the scrambling of no fewer than 15 of 252nd Squadron's aircraft in order to impress the opposite side sufficiently to let the trucks pass. However, the situation elsewhere was meanwhile beyond recovery and almost a week later, on 17 August 1991, MiG-21s from 117th Fighter Aviation Regiment, and G-4s from 252nd Fighter-Bomber Aviation Squadron, were sent to attack the prison facility in Stara Gradiška, which was meanwhile used as a base by the ZNG. It was during these operations that the remaining pilots of the RV i PVO were forced to realise that the Croats were well-informed about when and where they would fly. The solution was obvious and those flying slower J/IJ-21s and G-2s began violating the ban on flying at extremely low altitude. The risks involved in such operations became obvious on 20 August, when a pair of IJ-21s from 252nd Squadron came under fire over the town of Inđija, in eastern Slavonia. While evading fire, one of the jets hit a tree and tore off its wing-tip fuel tank and several 5-inch HVAR rockets. The pilot managed to nurse his badly damaged aircraft back to Batajnica.

The nose of this Jastreb aircraft from 240th Squadron, filmed in September 1991 at Mostar AB, had been repainted according to regulations on the removal of large white tactical numbers. (97th Brigade)

During the summer of 1991, the Moma Stanojlović plant received aircraft for repairs almost every day. Jastreb serial 24116 was damaged in a combat mission on 23 July. On 20 August, while on a video-reconnaissance mission, the pilot clipped a tree and the aircraft was severely damaged. The photograph from the plant shows the right wing that had been replaced. In the background is Jastreb serial 24213, which was damaged on August 21 by a hit to the left air intake from small arms fire. Jastreb serial 24116 was returned to 252nd Squadron on 18 September. It was shot down on 17 October. (VOC)

Withdrawal from threatened Air Bases

The general withdrawal of the JNA from Slovenia and the increasing pressure of the Croat forces prompted the leadership of the JNA into the conclusion that the situation of multiple air bases in Croatia had become untenable. Some units had already been withdrawn during the war in Slovenia, but this process was further accelerated in late June 1991. The first to go were Ka-25s, Ka-28s, and Mi-14s, which were evacuated from Divulje AB to Mostar on the 28th of that month – explained as enabling their 'more efficient combat use' and the 'securing of the rear.' Following a temporary stop in July, between 10 and 30 August 1991 the Command of the VVA was then evacuated by Mi-8s of 107th Mixed Aviation Regiment from Zemunik AB to Rajlovac, while its four regiments were directly subordinated to the commands of I and V Corps RV i PVO. Also during August, G-2s and G-4s of 249th Fighter-Bomber Aviation Squadron and 251st Fighter-Bomber Aviation Squadron from 105th Fighter-Bomber Aviation Regiment were transferred from Zemunik to Udbina AB, situated in the part of Lika 'comfortably' within the SAO Krajina. Therefore, for the time being, only the G-2s of 333rd Fighter-Bomber Aviation Squadron remained at Zemunik AB. Those elements of the Air Force Academy that were responsible for the theoretical part of the curriculum, and the battalion housing students were to follow to Rajlovac only once the fighting not only reached, but indeed overran Zadar.

The next to go were flying units from Pula AB. The command of 185th Fighter-Bomber Aviation Regiment was disbanded. Training of students continued for a while longer, but meanwhile, G-4s of 229th Fighter-Bomber Aviation Squadron were transferred to Golubovi AB and the unit was re-assigned to 172nd Fighter-Bomber Aviation Regiment. Similarly, MiG-21PFM/UMs of 129th Fighter Aviation Squadron were transferred to Tuzla AB. The latter facility had had no permanently assigned unit since Plan Jedinstvo, but was operated by 399th Air Base and included four runways (PSS-1, with a length of 2,470m and 12 HAS; PSS-2 with a length of 1,800m and 8 HAS, PSS-3 with 2,000m length and 8 HAS, and a grass runway).

Units home-based at Pleso and Lučko, both outside Zagreb, were to follow. All the An-26s of 679th Transport Aviation Squadron were transferred to Batajnica AB. Due to the lack of space at other air bases, the RV i PVO decided to reactivate Zalužani airfield outside Banja Luka. Constructed in 1955, the local grass runway was originally used for training pilots for piston-engined Yakovlev-interceptors, and subsequently by the local aero-club, while the barracks were used by armoured and mechanised units. When Zalužani was re-activated in 1991, it was initially occupied by the aerial technical service, and served as a workshop for tanks. Correspondingly, Gazelles from Lučko initially moved to Pleso AB, but were eventually temporarily deployed at Bihać AB, while Mi-8s of 780th Transport Helicopter Squadron were transferred directly to Zalužani. Finally, after realising that Bihać AB was now overcrowded, the Gazelles also followed to Zalužani, but in the process 713th Anti-Tank Helicopter Squadron was disbanded and merged into 711th Anti-Tank Helicopter Squadron.[3]

After a hit in the internal fuel tank, the pilot of Jastreb serial 24261 from 252nd Squadron had to land at Sombor airfield. Under the wing, a launcher can be seen in which only one of the 12 57mm rockets remains, along with an unfired HVAR rocket. Aircraft serial 24261 was originally an attack version but had a wing-tip tank with an aerial camera on the front. (Zdenko Molnar)

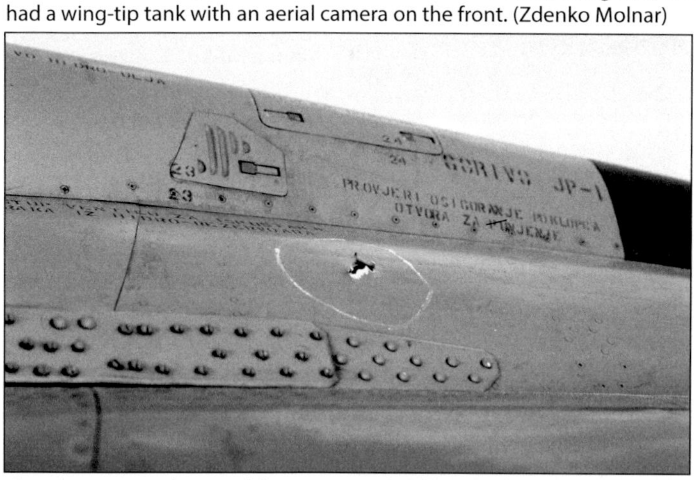

The penetration of a round from an assault rifle through the fuel tank of Jastreb serial 24261. (Zdenko Molnar)

It was embarrassing for the pilot of this Jastreb to see the punctures in the skin of the aircraft after returning from the mission. This was a common sight in the summer of 1991, when Jastreb aircraft flew low and were subjected to massive fire from assault rifles and machine guns. (Zdenko Molnar)

Removal of Tactical Numbers

As the SFRJ slowly slipped into the war, and the RV i PVO flew ever more combat sorties, some pilots began repainting their highly visible white helmets in July 1991, with 249th and 251st squadrons from Zemunik AB apparently being the first to do so. On 9 August, the air force then confirmed this practice with an official order, which specified the use of chromoden grey and olive-drab colours to camouflage the helmets. Moreover, the same order stipulated the removal of prominent white or black tactical numbers from all aircraft and helicopters and these were to be repainted in the same colours as the pilots' helmets. An exception were tactical numbers applied on the upper right wing, and the full, five-digit serial numbers on the vertical tail or cone. According to the order for this repainting procedure, care had to be taken of the existing camouflage scheme or rather that the new stains do not deviate from the colour around the mark. For aircraft that had their number applied in nitro colours, it was determined that this was first to be removed with thinner, and then overpainted with polyurethane colours. An exception to this rule were transport aircraft or types operated in small numbers, including An-26s, Yak-40s, Falcon 50s, and Learjet 25Bs.

Jastreb Down

Complete lack of interest in finding a compromise and the insistence of all the senior politicians in Croatia and Serbia of their version of events being the 'right' and 'good' one, and the unwillingness of the JNA to act, ensured that the tensions between the armed Croatian Serb and Croatian authorities continued escalating. Through August, exchanges of fire became a daily occurrence, even more so as the town of Vukovar was de-facto besieged by the Serbian militias from Slavonia, Serbian paramilitary forces from Serbia, and the JNA. The more often there was fighting on the ground, the more often the RV i PVO was called upon for assistance, and the more often its low-flying aircraft received ground fire.

On 21 August 1991, two Jastrebs were hit by the ZNG in Sarvaš and their pilots returned fire with machineguns and unguided rockets. On 22 August, six Jastrebs sustained damage, and a pilot of 252nd Squadron was forced to make an emergency landing at Sombor airport because his aircraft was leaking oil. His wingman's aircraft was equipped with a video camera and this captured a soldier of the ZNG shooting at the front Jastreb, but missing because he did not calculate the lead-time, and thus hit the second jet instead. The inevitable happened on 24 August 1991, when three Jastrebs from 252nd Fighter-Bomber Aviation Squadron were sent on a visual reconnaissance along the route Jankovci – Vinkovci – Vukovar at an altitude of 100 metres. Certainly

After a hit from a 20mm AAG on 24 August 1991 pilot Aćimović ejected from his Jastreb, while the pilots of two other Jastrebs circled and monitored the situation. The aero-photo camera of one of the aircraft recorded the scene and one image shows Aćimović`s parachute, while another shows local people running to help the pilot near the burning remains of the aircraft. (252nd Squadron)

enough, the pilots actually flew lower to keep themselves safe. Captain Saša Aćimović led the formation in J-21 serial number 24256 and was the first to spot several coaches – as frequently used to transport Croat forces at the time. Deciding to take a closer look, he turned right and flew around a grain silo, across the Đergajforest, and towards the entrance to the village of Bršadin. At that point in time, his jet received a hit from a 20mm M55 gun in the left intake area. With dense black smoke leaking out of the fuselage, Aćimović was left with no choice but to eject over the part of Bršadin controlled by the Serbs. After landing by parachute, he ran to the nearest houses that were a few hundred metres away and using a bicycle borrowed from one of the inhabitants, Aćimović then reached Borovo Selo in time to be picked up by a helicopter that then returned him to Batajnica AB.

Later on, the Serbs found out that Aćimović's jet was shot down by the gunner named Luka Andrijanić, who joined the ZNG at the age of 19, immediately after concluding his service with the JNA as an operator of a M55 gun at Batajnica AB. His gun was positioned atop a grain silo in the Croat-controlled part of Bršadin. Only a month later, Andrijanić was killed while setting up anti-tank mines.

Since the beginning of the conflict in Slovenia the number of An-26 flights, which played a key role in maintaining links with bases in the western part of SFRJ, drastically declined. Two An-26s from 379th Squadron (71369 and 71377), which were transferred from Pleso IAP, and guest aircraft 71356 from Niš`s 677th Squadron, were photographed at Batajnica AB during the first half of September. (Mladen Savić)

Stormy Days

From the Croatian point of view, the complete aerial domination by the RV i PVO during the summer of 1991 was a huge problem. As the local historians later wrote in relation to the battle for Vukovar, the actions of the air force were both 'very successful and deadly' and the Croatian troops were 'powerless in the face of this power and force.' Indeed, 'the lethality of air strikes led to the demoralisation of not only the fighters, but also the civilian population.' This was even more so the case because by 25 August 1991, the JNA began openly deploying its mechanised units against the ZNG in eastern Slavonia, exercising so much pressure that the Croats usually lacked the time for post-operational debriefs and analysis and they were only able to count their dead and wounded, or realise that somebody was missing, and then to write off equipment that was lost or destroyed.[4] The situation further worsened when, during the last week of August, the air force further intensified its CAS operations in response to requests of the ground forces. By then, and contrary to the situation from the previous two months, pilots no longer flew combat air patrols and relatively little reconnaissance, instead they were sent directly into ground attacks.

On 25 August 1991, it was the turn of 126th Fighter Aviation Squadron to fly its first combat sorties of the war. A day later, this unit and 252nd Squadron, flew a series of strikes against the positions of the ZNG and police in Vukovar, Borovo Naselje, and Sotina. Moreover, two MiG-21bis emptied their Munja launchers for 57mm unguided rockets at the silo in Bršadin. The Croats fired back with everything that was available, and both a J-21 from the 252nd, and a MiG-21bis from 117th Fighter Aviation Regiment suffered light damage.

Due to the high risk at Pleso AB and Lučko airfiled, Gazelle helicopters flew to Bihać and were temporarily accommodated on runway Number 5, which could be used for take-off but not landing of MiG-21 aircraft. (Mladen Savić)

In the summer of 1991, in addition to occasional combat tasks, the RV i PVO mainly flew routine training. On 29 August, Captain Danilo Milić and Captain Zoran Drljača took off from Banja Luka AB with two-seater NJ-22 Orao 25505. On the way back to the airport, the right leg of the main landing gear would not come out. The pilots tried to solve the problem while their fuel lasted and then they had to eject. They directed the aircraft towards a hill away from the settlement, five kilometres from the runway threshold. The pilots escaped without injuries. (117th Brigade)

On 26 August, two G-4s were dispatched to provide CAS for 221st Motorised Brigade in fighting for the village of Kijevo in Dalmatia. At around 0900hrs, they rocketed two roadblocks on the road to Sinj, when one was slightly damaged by ground fire. Nevertheless, their strike enabled the Serb infantry to enter and then capture Kijevo.

A day later, the air force suffered its next war-related loss, when MiG-21R serial number 26102 was written off. Lieutenant Roman Džalev took off from Bihać AB at 2025hrs, as a fourth in formation, for a routine training mission over western Bosnia. Suddenly, radio contact to him was lost and then the wreckage of his aircraft was found on the western side of Mount Plješevica, above his home base.

Meanwhile, the combination of a series of attacks by Serb militias and paramilitary forces, and the Croat siege of a local JNA base resulted in what the hardliners in both Croatia and Serbia were looking for: an open battle for the town of Vukovar. The Croat forces were commanded by two defectors: Major Mile 'Jastreb' Dedaković, a former pilot and officer at HQ 5th MD, specialised in aerial surveillance, and Captain Branko 'Mladi Jastreb' Borković, who used to serve with 155th Air Defence Rocket Regiment. Theoretically, the RV i PVO was covering the Vukovar area with nearly every type in operational service, including G-2s, G-4s, J-21s, and Mig-21s. However, when, on 30 August 1991, an IJ-21 of 252nd Squadron, equipped with Vinten cameras, returned from a reconnaissance sortie of Mikanovci railway station with photographs showing the Croats unloading arms and ammunition from railway cars and re-loading it on to trucks, instead of ordering an attack, the air force banned all further flying operations over this zone.[5]

Operation Ajkula: Interception and Confiscation of a Boeing 707

In the early morning hours of 31 August, a Boeing 707-324C cargo aircraft wearing markings of Uganda Airlines Cargo, registration number 5X-UCM, landed at Pleso IAP. The 'Follow Me' vehicle took the aircraft to the tarmac on the eastern side of the airport, which was still controlled by the JRV i PVO. The aircraft was surrounded by military vehicles and BRDM-2 scout cars, and by members of 63rd Parachute Brigade. After a short stand off the crew – who were of Kenyan nationality – came out, accompanied by Antun Kikaš, a Canadian businessman of Croat origin. Kikaš was then confronted by Colonel Bajić from V Corps RV i PVO, who requested him to hand over his documents and those for the cargo carried by the aircraft – which was then subjected to a thorough inspection. There, the JNA troops found a total of 520 South-African-made 5.56mm R4 assault rifles with 621,000 rounds of ammunition, and 1,350 75mm HEAT R1M3 rifle grenades. According to the cargo manifest, the total weight was 19,176kg and worth US$1,136,000. Rather unsurprisingly, the JNA charged the crew and the sole passenger with arms smuggling. They were put under arrest and flown out in a single Mi-8 to Bihać AB, and from there by an An-26 to Batajnica AB, for further investigation and prosecution.

The grounding of the Ugandan aircraft was preceded by a story in which the interests of intelligence services and arms traders intertwined. Kikaš had initiated a fund-raising campaign amongst the Croats in Canada to purchase arms and because of bad experiences with financial aid collected in that way much too often ending up in the pockets of top Croat politicians (including Tuđman), Kikaš ran the entire operation personally. As first, he established contacts with the Croat authorities, who secured the support of the Service for Protection of the Constitutional Order. Then, 'armed' with a suitcase stuffed full of about US$1 million, he went searching for suitable arms dealers. In Vienna, capital of Austria, he met people that forwarded him to Frankfurt, in Germany, and then to a British arms dealer based in Johannesburg in the Republic of South Africa. From Johannesburg, Kikaš then travelled to Pretoria, to meet representatives of the South African Ministry of Defence and receive their 'green light' for the acquisition and transfer of armament. The plan was to fly with the cargo across Africa and to request a technical landing at Brnik airport, Ljubljana. The reception of the cargo was planned, in cooperation with Croatian and Slovenian secret services, with six trucks for the transport of the cargo to Croatia.

On 29 August the chartered Boeing flew from Entebbe in Uganda to Gaborone in Botswana and then to Mmbatho (at that time the capital of the so-called Bantustan, today a part of the Republic of South Africa) where the cargo was loaded. The next step in the concealment of the traces of the illicit transfer of armament was the return of the loaded aircraft to Entebbe where a new cargo manifest was issued on 30 August. A series of indicators suggested to Kikaš that there would be problems – the pilot was replaced without explanation. The new pilot, Stephen Michieli, did not have all the information and did not know that it was planned that an emergency landing would be reported. Only once in the air did Michieli learn that he was to fly to the central part of the Adriatic Sea, supposedly to Trieste in the north-eastern part of Italy, and then request a landing at Brnik airport once he was in Slovenian air space in the area of Ilirska Bistrica. Once the Boeing 707 had entered the area of jurisdiction of the Yugoslav ATC over the Adriatic Sea he was asked routine questions. In response to questions about the precise cargo being carried was advised by Kikaš to report "general cargo". Michieli made a mistake in communicating with the controller and said that they were flying to Ljubljana, which was closed by the Yugoslav authorities. The controller informed the pilot that he could not go to that destination and should immediately leave Yugoslav air space. Kikaš decided to say that they were heading to Vienna, but in the meantime, the controller had informed the pilot that he should continue to Ljubljana. At that moment the Boeing 707 was above the Adriatic Sea, approximately in the vicinity of Dubrovnik. Kikaš demanded that the pilot continue over the sea, but the pilot followed the orders of the control and entered deep into Yugoslavia. He was informed that Ljubljana was closed for technical reasons and that they were to go to Pleso airport. In the meantime, V Corps RV i PVO command post was ordered to intercept the Boeing 707.

During this time the base at Bihać put a pair of MiG-21bis aircraft from 124th FAS into standby mode with pilots in the aircraft. The thick morning fog headed toward the runways of the base and it was certain that the conditions were not safe for flying. After more than half an hour of waiting, the pilots left the aircraft.

The base at Pula did have acceptable meteorological conditions for take-off where there were two MiG-21PFM aircraft on QRA. One of these was piloted by Boriša Mandić who recalled that the morning shifts at that base, from 0400 to 0600hrs, were the 'hardest stuff' as during the transition of night-to-day he had difficulties staying awake. His shift-colleague was Dragan Grubeša. Both pilots wore the ranks of Captain 1st Class and were experienced senior flight instructors in 129th Fighter-Aviation Squadron. Mandić remembers the voice of the deputy commander of his unit waking him up from a sound sleep:

> I was awakened by a penetrating voice in the corridor – two in the air, Banja Luka (area of the mission), 10 thousand meters. I looked at my watch – 04.20hrs. I quickly grabbed my helmet, tablet, chart, anti-G suit, lifebelt. While I was putting on my anti-G suit, besides my aircraft, the leader of the technical team informed me that the APA was broken (ground mobile electrical unit on a truck) and that we could not carry out the mission. The technicians did not

A MiG-21PFM from 129th FAS, a unit for training fighter pilots, as used to intercept the Boeing 707. (Aleksandar Radić)

The commander of 129th FAS Lieutenant Colonel Zoran Ilić congratulating his pilot Boriša Mandić on successfully forcing the Boeing 707 to land. In the background is a MiG-21PFM with two R-3S air-to-air missiles under its wings. (Boriša Mandić collection)

believe that we were going on a real mission of interception of the 'blue team'. We started the engines with the aircraft's batteries, with the risk of malfunction and destruction of batteries because that wasn't the usual procedure for a MiG-21 aircraft. Those 80-90 seconds needed for the engine to come out to regime 'idling' were an eternity for me. Grubeša was the first to start his engines and roll out to start 09. We respected radio silence and communicated only with visual signs. The meteorological situation could not have been worse, and daylight had not broken the early morning greyness in the base that was close to the sea. Horizontal visibility was around two kilometres vertically and laterally – much less than required for the take-off of a pair of MiGs on a regime of full afterburner. Grubeša took the left position of the leader of the pair on the runway and freed the right side of take-off for me. Immediately after taking off, and before the retracting of the landing gear, we entered into the dark greyness. The visibility was low and the only way I could see and maintain the position in the pair was by the flames of the afterburner on the leader's exhaust. I tried to at least see the flag on the vertical tail and determine the position of my aircraft with the leader. I couldn't let myself go to the right and break up the pair. The climbing had dragged on and in the absence of a realistic estimate of time passing, at one moment I thought we were over Hungary. We did not identify ourselves to ground control from Pleso because the codes seemed to have changed and we moved to open test in communication, we switched the channel and had contact with the guidance officer. By voice, I recognized who the officer was and reservations towards the security of the mission were rejected. We followed the instructions carefully. We arrived at the area and the altitude where visibility was much better. For easier visual observation of the front hemisphere, I took the spaced order and switched on the radar to the 'observation' mode. Due to too many false reflections, I dimmed the radar screen and prepared a K-13 missile. On a slight left turn at an altitude of about 6,000 meters and a speed of about 800 km/h we received information from the guidance officer: 'Blue is below you, upon establishing visual contact, monitoring is active, and if non-compliance .... action was suggested'. Keeping the aircraft of the leader constantly in my sector of peripheral sight, I focused my eyes down, left and 60 ° forward for a moment – I could clearly see the 'blue', a large four-engine white aircraft, occasionally disappearing in the grey and white haze. Making turns above the 'blue' I easily established that it was a Boeing 707, but I did not see the windows of the passenger cabin and characteristic white shirts of pilots. My first thought was that this was a remote-controlled aircraft. If we shoot it down and it falls to the ground, there may be many innocent victims. My suspicion was even stronger when I read Uganda Airlines on the fuselage without a visible registration or flag. Only on the ground did I see that it was a windowless cargo aircraft and that the pilots were Africans in black overalls. For several minutes we followed the 'blue' in the turns above it and constant descent towards Pleso airport. Due to a large difference in progressive velocities, we had to make turns with larger radius with occasional arrival and hold in the rear semi-sphere of the 'blue'. In those moments, I heard in my headphones the very well known sound of the infrared K-13 missile due to the large radiance of energy from the Boeing's four engines. At an altitude of around 2,000 meters, we lost contact

The Boeing 707 at Batajnica AB, photographed after the flight from Pleso AB and before the repainting of the Uganda Airlines markings. (Zdenko Molnar)

As a reward for the interception of the Boeing 707, pilot Mandić received one of the R4 assault rifles that were found in the aircraft. Mandić is seen here posing in front of the Boeing 707 at Pula AB in autumn 1991. (Milorad Ristić)

Subsequent investigation revealed that the pilot of the Boeing 707 saw both interceptors and was never in any dilemma over whether to follow their instructions and land as advised. On the ground, the Croat authorities were seriously considering ordering an assault, however, they gave up because they estimated that the defences of the base were too strong and that the risk was too great.

Around half an hour after the event at Pleso airport, another pair of MiG-21PFM aircraft took off from Pula on the interception of a Tupolev Tu-154 airliner of the Romanian TAROM. After being forced to land for inspection at Pleso IAP, this aircraft was permitted to continue its voyage.

with the "blue" due to cloudiness and after several minutes from an altitude of 1,000 meters, I saw Pleso. On the landing approach, I took a look at our 'blue'. We were instructed by our guidance officer to continue with the turn over the airport. Due to the long regime of afterburner during take-off and climbing and the relatively long tailing of the 'blue', fuel reserves were minimal. The MiG-21PFM fuel gauge goes wrong even up to 300 litres. I feared that the engine would stop working and that I would have to eject above the territory where we were 'not liked', so therefore I asked several times for permission to land. Each time, I received a resolute response 'negative'. In the left turn over Pleso airport, we followed the flow of events. After landing and parking on the military platform, our 'blue' was blocked with armoured vehicles. We finally received the ok for landing. A few times during the taxiing I received an order to immediately vacate the link to the runway and platform because blue colour armoured vehicles (note BOV-M) of the Croatian Ministry of the interior were driving towards from the civilian part of the airport intending to destroy the 707.

In the meantime, around 1400hrs, the Federal air traffic control closed air space over Croatia and Slovenia. In the time from 1454 to 1507hrs four DC-9s of Adria Airways and one DC-9 of Yugoslav Air Transport (Jugoslovenski Air Transport, JAT) took off from Brnik airport: Slovenian Adria aircraft flew over the Karavanks mountains to Klagenfurt in Austria. Tailing the first DC-9 was a Galeb-4 aircraft, which did not commence aggressive action, but the crew of the DC-9 made a steep climb to cross the border as soon as possible. The second Galeb-4 aircraft made a sweeping flight over the runway and control tower.

The MiG-21 pilots involved named their mission Operation Ajkula after the radio-call-signs of their 129th Squadron. Correspondingly, they planned to launch Operation Ajkula-2 – escort of the Boeing 707 – while this was underway to Batajnica AB. The lack of fuel for the cargo jet proved to be a problem and the crew informed the officers of the RV i PVO that there was only enough fuel on board for a flight of 20 minutes. The air force logistics had no fuel tanker with a high-pressure filling port. Eventually, the air force then requested help from the Croat civilian authorities, but these only deployed various vehicles to block the main runway of the airport.

During 31 August MiG-21bis aircraft from 117th Fighter Aviation Regiment flew CAPs over Pleso, circling in half-hour shifts, two aircraft at a time – one armed with two R-3R missiles and two R-60s, and the other with two UB-16-57 or Munja launchers for unguided rockets.

The next day, 1 September, a Falcon 50 arrived at Pleso carrying Prime Minister Marković. For his arrival, the runway was cleared for a few minutes, and this opportunity was promptly exploited to scramble the two MiG-21PFMs from the taxiway on the military side and return to Pula. It was only after extensive negotiations that Pleso was re-opened and the Boeing 707 refuelled and then transferred to Batajnica AB on 5 September. By then the Federal authorities handed the aircraft to the RV i PVO, where it received the serial number 73601. For its operations, the air force mobilised crews of the JAT (which used to fly Boeing 707s until November 1987) and reserve officer pilots had to quickly resume training because the aircraft was urgently needed for missions between the bases in the western SFRJ and Batajnica. The RV i PVO had entered the war without high-capacity aircraft and its sole An-12B was withdrawn from service in November 1990. The planned procurement of the L-100-30 Hercules was not completed and the 43-tonne payload of the 707 was therefore highly appreciated. During the last weeks of the conflict in Croatia alone, it carried 2,387 people and 767 tons of cargo in 117 flights. The assault rifles from the SAR mainly became the property of 63rd Parachute Brigade, and thus remained with the RV i PVO.

5 COUNTER-AIR OPERATIONS

In the incidents during the summer of 1991 pilots of combat aircraft most frequently flew at low altitudes, often following selected roads or railroads. Indeed, experiences from this period had proven low altitude strikes to be the most effective tactics, despite the inevitable entry of the aircraft into the envelope of light infantry weapons. Most targets were positioned along the Croat line of control and not a single air strike is known to have ever been launched against any of the Serbian militias or paramilitary groups active in Croatia during the summer and autumn of 1991. The most critical phases of every mission were the arrival over the target, the passage through the usual hail of machinegun and assault rifle fire, and then the exit from the combat zone. Occasional incidents between Croatia and Serbia during the summer of 1991 were becoming more frequent. Units of the JNA were under pressure from Croats and gradually soldiers got accustomed to daily firing of weapons, mainly as a show of force. The incidents turned into all-out battles and the JNA openly supported the Serb militias.

No specific date has ever been defined as the starting point of the war. Even in August, the JNA became directly involved against the Croats only in two areas: around Vukovar and in Dalmatia. In other parts of Croatia, nervous peace prevailed. Yet, from mid-August 1991 the RV i PVO began flying what were called 'free hunting operations' in its jargon, and thus it can be said that the air war had a very clear starting date.

Beginnings of Sectarianism: Kurjaci sa Ušća

On 18 August 1991, two IJ-21 Jastrebs and several pilots of 354th Reconnaissance Aviation Squadron were re-assigned to 252nd Fighter-Bomber Squadron to bolster the unit for operations over eastern Slavonia. During the following days, and in order to maintain security of the mission, the commander of the latter unit began issuing his orders orally to selected pilots, and then without specifying the target, he would only name the combat zone in question. In turn, squadron commanders relied on intelligence reports, foremost based on reconnaissance operations. And thus the RV i PVO began flying free hunting operations. This method of fighting imposed a heavy burden upon pilots as not only were the targets not pre-determined, causing problems with calculation of the necessary fuel, but even the overall objective of their efforts was unclear. One of the squadron-commanders at the time defined the issue 'We did not know what

The main zone in which the Galeb-4 jets from 252nd Squadron operated was East Slavonia, a region in the Pannonian plain. Under combat conditions the aircraft would have flown in a much more dispersed formation with several hundred metres between them. (Dragan Veličković)

The commander of 252nd Squadron, Lieutenant Colonel Života Marković, in the control tower of Banja Luka AB. It was under his firm leadership that a squadron that had 40 aircraft in August 1991 carried out 989 combat missions that year. (252nd Squadron)

Lieutenant Colonel Marković conducting a pre-take off inspection of a Galeb-4 aircraft at Banja Luka AB in the summer of 1991. (252nd Squadron)

our mission was, nor why were we flying: were we fighting for the preservation of Yugoslavia? Why were we tolerating the breakup of the country?'

The probable reason for this change of tactics was the fact that so far, and for all practical purposes, the air force was hardly utilised in the war and also that there was a 'growing desire to do more' within its ranks. In the RV i PVO before the war, ordering air strikes was a matter of necessity: commanders of ground and naval units of the JNA, respectively, or of the TO, would plan aerial support depending on the type of action expected. During the war in Slovenia, forward air controllers were deployed with numerous units that had attempted to reach various border crossings but rarely called for air strikes. In Croatia in the summer of 1991, there was no forward air control at all.

In attempt to improve its target selection, the command of 252nd Fighter-Bomber Aviation Squadron decided to organise a team that would monitor radio traffic in the combat zone. Whilst a request for the provision of suitable equipment was ignored by the security service of the RV i PVO it was not ignored by the State Security Service (Služba državne bezbednosti, SDB) or the Serbian MUP. Both of these agencies were already involved neck-deep in organising and supporting the formation of multiple Serbian paramilitary units – especially so in Dalmatia and eastern Slavonia. To them, it was very opportune that 252nd Squadron showed its preparedness to operate more intensively and indeed, together with several other units of the RV i PVO recognised as having a 'high concentration of ethnic Serbs', it was expected to be particularly determined in the fighting. Recalling the nick name of the first-ever flying squadron of the Serbian armed forces – Kurjaci sa Ušća – the unit began using this designation. Indeed, although at the time unit insignia was not officially permitted in the RV i PVO (they were considered to impair security), pilots of 252nd Squadron began applying chevrons on their overalls. The unit thus quickly established itself as in possession of a 'special status' in the air force, and found itself subordinated directly to the Command of I Corps RV i PVO – while de-facto losing contact with the Command of 97th Aviation Brigade, although still nominally assigned to it.[1]

Emboldened, on 31 August 1991, the commander of 252nd Fighter-Bomber Aviation Squadron, Lieutenant-Colonel Života Marković, wrote a letter to the Command I Corps RV i PVO, requesting intensified participation of his unit, and emphasising that his pilots were ready to hit back, especially if one of them might get shot down over Croatia: '....we are urging our military leadership to act reasonably as soon as possible!'

A day later all pilots from this unit were summoned by Major-General Jurjević, who questioned them about the large number of small-arms hits on their aircraft. His position was that they should usually fly at an altitude of 700 metres, never below 100-200 metres, and never outside radio range. Moreover, he reminded everybody, that a pilot's job was not to run politics.

The Hunt for An-2s

During the summer of 1991 the RV i PVO began receiving a growing amount of intelligence about ever larger arms smuggling operations into Croatia. In an atmosphere of omni-present paranoia, a myth emerged according to which Antonov An-2s of the agricultural aviation were deployed to carry ammunition from Hungary. The air force thus launched an all-out attempt to stop such flights – although having no confirmation that they took place at all – while its intelligence service was working hard to identify the airfields from which such flights took place. On 2 August, the 'daily internal information' was that such aircraft were all gathered at Pribislavec aero-club airport, outside Varaždin. In reality, no such operations were being undertaken but eight An-2s of the Agrar Aviation Osijek (Privredna avijacija Osijek, PA Osijek) had been transferred from their home-base of Čepin in eastern Croatia, to Pribislavec. Correspondingly, on 3 August 1991, G-4s from 252nd Squadron's detachment forward deployed at Banja Luka undertook their first attack on the grass runway near Varaždin, after approaching at low altitude to avoid detection. The mission was completed without problem, but no targets were found.

Nevertheless, related reports never stopped. Indeed, according to a subsequent report by the SSNO, from 20 August 1991, and for the

A Galeb-4 armed with a launcher for 128mm L-128-04 rockets. On the central under-fuselage pylon is a pod for a GSh-23 gun. (252nd Squadron)

On 3 August, a Galeb-4 from 252nd Squadron overflew Varaždin airfiled**,** at low altitude in a show of power. The aircraft took off from Banja Luka AB on an armed-reconnaissance mission loaded with two L128-04 pods for 128mm unguided rockets and a gun pod. Two additional 625-litre fuel tanks were necessary due to the length of the flight. A typical tactical radius for a Galeb-4 in a lo-lo-lo flight profile was 300 km, and the distance between Banja Luka and Varaždin was around 180 km. (Josip Novak)

following 20 days, 19 flights of 'agricultural' An-2s 'modified to transport up to 1.5 tonnes of arms and ammunition' had been registered. Another report on 6 September indicated an 'air bridge' organised between Varaždin and Nagykanizsa airport in Hungary, including at least one helicopter of the Hungarian Air Force. Moreover, at 2040hrs on 7 September 1991, several An-2s were supposed to have landed at Čepin after a low flight along the Danube River.

Indeed, reconnaissance overflights that evening finally managed to confirm the unloading of freight of unknown origin and nature from 10 An-2s and 2 Dromaders at Čepin. This prompted the JRV i PVO to decide to hunt down and destroy all such aircraft on the ground. Correspondingly, the jets of the Kurjaci sa Ušća attacked the Croat airfield on 3, 7, and 8 September. As far as is known, their strikes were successful in only one case, when the An-2 registered as YU-BHU, was destroyed.[2]

On 9 September 1991, 252nd Squadron changed its tactics. It transferred two J-21s and two G-2s from Batajnica to Sombor AB. This airfield had a runway of only 1,200 metres length (constructed by the Luftwaffe in 1944) but was only 10 kilometres from the Danube River and thus the border with Croatia. As such, it was an ideal forward operating base for attempts to intercept any An-2s coming low

A line of An-2s that flew to Varaždin from Osijek, on 2 August, recorded a day later. In the air attack on 15 September, aircraft YU-BOZ was completely destroyed, and the two neighbouring An-2s were damaged beyond economic repair. (Josip Novak)

over the river from the direction of Hungary. After sunset, the J-21 pilots scrambled to start their search for the Antonovs but found nothing and returned to Batajnica AB. The following night they developed their tactics even further when a G-2 deployed two SAB-100MN flare bombs, while a J-21 followed to intercept anything that might be detected. However, as soon as the first bomb was deployed, the two jets received fierce anti-aircraft fire, and their pilots could see nothing but a section of the Danube River. Disappointed, they returned to Batajnica. Moreover, the Hungarian government in Budapest issued a strong protest against activities close to its border. This effort was subsequently abandoned, although the ŠVK continued emphasising its official position that Hungary was directly involved in supplying armament to Croatia, and even enabling Croatian armed forces to use its airports.[3]

This 'Hunt for the An-2s' was subsequently re-directed against other airfields. On 15 September 1991, J-21 pilots of 240th Fighter-Bomber Aviation Squadron rocketed the airport of Start Grad on the island of Hvar. In their first sortie, they hit the runway with unguided rockets, and then used machine guns to destroy two Air Tractor AT-401 agricultural aircraft (property of PA Zagreb) and damage another, and two containers for the accommodation of personnel and equipment. Certainly enough, this was a highly effective attack as the aircraft in question had been modified to carry home-made 5kg and 10kg bombs and were in the process of being used to train their pilots to deploy these in combat.

Remains of An-2 YU-BOZ, destroyed by a Galeb-4 at Varaždin airfield. (Josip Novak)

Remains of An-2 YU-BFS, destroyed at Čepin airfield. (Nenad Šetina)

Hungarian Mi-8 helicopters, frequently active in the vicinity of the border with SFRJ on various assignments to control the border. They had a characteristic white recognition marking on the rear part of the fuselage. (Laszlo Javor)

Failed Acquisition of Mil Mi-24s

Early combat experiences from Slovenia and Croatia prompted the RV i PVO to search for ways to acquire Mil Mi-24 (ASCC/NATO-codename 'Hind') helicopter gunships. This led to negotiations with Moscow launched sometime in July 1991 and which continued into the following month. Indeed, on 6 August 1991, the Command of the RV i PVO ordered 16 pilots and 42 technical officers and other ranks to prepare for a one-month Russian-language course, 'with the goal of prompt preparations for conversion training and introduction to service' of an unnamed helicopter type. The unit selected to receive Mi-24s was to be a newly established squadron of 119th Aviation Brigade, home-based in Niš. However, this acquisition never took place: political turbulence in Moscow following a failed coup attempt – recklessly supported by Serbian officials – meant that, once back in power, the legal Soviet government refused to complete the deal. Any remaining hopes for such a deal were buried once the UN Security Council issued its Resolution 713, on 25 September 1991, which imposed an arms embargo upon the entire SFRJ, including Croatia, Slovenia, and all the follow-up republics.

Pribislavec airport was hit again on 15 September 1991, this time by MiG-21bis from Bihać AB. The shrapnel from their unguided rockets pierced the fuel tanks of an An-2 registered as YU-BOZ, which subsequently burned out. Several other aircraft of PA Osijek lined up nearby were all damaged, two of which – YU-BBN and YU-BFP – had to be decommissioned when the Croats realised that repairs would be unprofitable. Theoretically, the rest of the fleet was thus in deep trouble. However, on 16 September 1991, the Hungarian authorities granted permission for their evacuation over the border and a day later the surviving five An-2s, two Cessna 172s, and one Utva-75 were then flown to the Murska Sobota airfield instead. The RV i PVO did attempt to intercept them, but a pair of MiG-21s scrambled from Bihać AB arrived over Varaždin very late. Jastrebs attacked Pribislavec airfield near Čakovec and heavily damaged an old Soko 522 training aircraft, which stood there as the gate guardian.

Slightly more successful was the last known air strike on Čepin airfield, undertaken on 19 September and which resulted in the destruction of the An-2s YU-BFS and YU-BOC, and the Dromader YU-BNS.

6
ALL-OUT WAR

In the first half of September 1991, the propaganda war between not only Belgrade and Zagreb, but indeed between the JNA and the Croats, reached frenzy level. Both sides accused the other of aggressive action, day after day. In reality Croatia was still on the strategic defensive, and its armed forces still unable to run any kind of serious offensive operations. On the contrary, the Serb militias from Croatia and paramilitary forces from Serbia were meanwhile deeply involved in attacking the separatist-controlled republic – meanwhile with open support of the JNA. Once again, the developments on the ground prompted the RV i PVO into changing its tactics from that of flying 'free hunt' operations, into providing CAS following a well-coordinated plan with the ground forces, i.e. on-call by the Yugoslav National Army. This practice in turn forced the air force to keep a large number of fully armed and fully fuelled jets on alert, with pilots in their cockpits, ready to take-off at short notice. The land forces of JNA and the RV i PVO had meanwhile continued their withdrawal from Slovenia and Croatia, which included the families of the military personnel. Oddly enough, routine training sorties were still undertaken – often deep inside the Croat airspace. On 5 September 1991, Captain Neša Vrangelovski took off from Zemunik AB for training with a Kub-M SAM-site on the coast. However, once over the sea, he most likely suffered from spatial disorientation and hit the calm surface.[1]

Ground Fire Everywhere

In action almost everywhere along nearly 1,000-kilometres of frontlines that gradually came into being along the eastern and southern borders of Croatia, helicopter-crews of the RV i PVO experienced numerous harrowing adventures. On 8 September, a Mi-8 involved in the evacuation of two JNA troops was fired upon by the Croats over Okučani, in western Slavonia, although they had been informed in time about the nature of its mission. Two days later, another Mi-8 was damaged while underway in the area of Paklenica. On 11 September, a third Mi-8 over Okučani suffered hits to the fuel tank while transporting a representative of the ECCM supposed to witness the signing of a local ceasefire agreement, while a fourth was damaged while overflying the strategically important Maslenica Bridge in northern Dalmatia. Also on 11 September, a Mi-8 from 890th Medium Helicopter Squadron was hit by ground fire while trying to resupply the besieged base of 12th Proletarian Mechanised Brigade in Osijek. Gazelles were at least as present, and the example with the serial number 12606 from 849th Reconnaissance and Liaison Squadron carrying Major-General Milan Aksentijević – assistant commander of 5th MD for moral and legal matters – famous for being the last representative of the JNA to the Slovenian Parliament – was hit by rifle fire while underway in the area of Slunjska Brda in central Croatia. The crew, consisting of Lieutenant-Colonel Veljko Leka and Captain 1st Class Zoran Babić managed to land safely near the village of Tušilović, 13km south of Karlovac, in an area controlled by the Croatian Serbs. Determined to continue to Zagreb, and self-conscious of his fame, Aksentijević then took

A Galeb-2 from 252nd Squadron on a combat mission over east Slavonia, armed with two 5-inch HVAR rockets, as photographed by the reconnaissance camera of another jet. (252nd Squadron)

War in East Slavonia. JNA soldiers and an M-60PB APC on the Dalj – Borovo Selo road in 1991. (Borba)

Jastreb jets from 240th Squadron were armed with 5-inch HVAR unguided rockets and a bundle of 16kg RAB-16 bombs, which were converted 120mm mortar shells. (97th Brigade)

One of the two-seat NJ-21 Jastrebs from 240th Squadron was photographed in preparation for a combat mission. A technician is loading a launcher for 57mm rockets and a solider is fuelling the aircraft. (97th Brigade)

a Puch 4WD of the TO and, continued escorted by two M86 armoured vehicles. Rather unsurprisingly, he was stopped at a checkpoint of the Croat Lučko anti-terror unit while entering Karlovac and arrested together with his bodyguards. On 25 November, Aksentijević was exchanged for Kikaš, the Canadian businessman arrested when the Boeing 707 carrying a load of South African assault rifles was impounded at Pleso IAP on 31 August. The damaged Gazelle was initially scheduled for destruction but was then recovered to Bihać AB, repaired, and returned to service.

During a mission over Vukovar on 14 September, J-21 serial number 24133 was a hit by ground fire and Lieutenant-Colonel Miodrag Dautovic was badly wounded:

> I was at a low altitude in the turn above Mitnica (a district in Vukovar; author's note). Suddenly, a blunt sound came from the left side. I felt severe pain in the area below my left ribs and pulled the aircraft to a higher altitude. It was clear to me that I was a hit. I straightened the slope and looked into the instrument panel. The engine was working normally, and instruments indicated usual positions. I felt warmth on the left side of my chest and noticed a bloody stain on the flight suit that was spreading. For a moment it seemed like I was running out of air. I set the oxygen lever to maximum flow. The chest pain was getting worse. I am moving the throttle to maximum position ... Due to the deadly ordnance under the wings, the aircraft seems to fly slowly. I felt like vomiting. I fly and my eyes are shut ... I am contacting the flight control even though I can't hear myself. I say that I am injured and I am asking for the runway to be cleared ... Hand movements are getting harder and I still have to pull out the landing gear ... When I realized that with the ordnance that I hadn't dropped I had to land softly and precisely, it was as if the pain had intensified ... It is time to pull out the landing gear. I'm gritting my teeth ... the pain makes me want to vomit. I squint and touch. I reached for the handle and pulled it towards me ... I listen to the beats. If the gear is not damaged I need to hear three. One, two...three! I am relieved. I can see the runway, but it kind of

shifts from left to right ... now I cannot squint anymore because I won't have a second chance. I took away the throttle. Lined up with the runway ... I didn't even feel the touch. I am sure that I have never before landed so softly and accurately.[2]

Dautović was wounded in the chest by pieces of a 12.7 mm round which punctured the fuselage on the right side. After this experience, pilots began regularly wearing ballistic vests they obtained from the ground forces.

In addition to aircraft of 252nd Fighter-Bomber Squadron, MiG-21s from 126th Fighter Aviation Squadron were also active over Vukovar on 14 September. Indicative of the intensity of operations was the fact that they flew a total of seven missions as pairs and eight as a trio, firing a total of 12 S-24B, 256 S-57K and 48 128mm unguided rockets. Less effective was an Orao pilot from 242nd Fighter-Bomber Squadron who, due to a navigational error – being a flier familiar with Bosnian mountains but not with the flat Panonian Plain – bombed the village of Bač in northern Serbia, instead of the silo in Đergaj, killing three civilians and wounding nine.

Kadijević's Plan

As of mid-September 1991, dozens of JNA units were blocked inside their barracks deep within Croatia, while ever more units were re-deployed from other parts of Yugoslavia into eastern and central Croatia. As they became involved in a true myriad of clashes, the ŠVK realised that it was losing control of the situation. Indeed, command and control became exceptionally problematic, although – at least in theory – run along a relatively simple chain of command. The Presidency of the SFRJ (in which the presidents rotated according to a pre-established scheme, so that the representative of every federal unit served a one-year mandate) exercised the function of a Commander-in-Chief. The SIV exercised administrative control over the entire armed forces, while the strategic level commands – 1st, 3rd and 5th MDs, the Naval Military District and the RV i PVO – were subordinated to both the presidency and the SSNO. In reality, the division within the presidency not only compromised the very presidency, but the position of the SSNO. Dissatisfied with the attitude of political leaders regarding the preservation of the SFRJ, the generals of the ŠVK acted, essentially, on their own – both with regards to combat operations, and as a separate political body. This problem culminated in May 1991, when the Croatian representative to the Presidency of the SFRJ, Stipe Mesić, began his term as President. From the standpoint of the senior officers of the JNA, this was a heresy and the title of the Supreme Commander was now with an open opponent of Yugoslavia. Unsurprisingly, the generals attempted to block even his election to that position. However, on 1 July, and under immense pressure from the international community, Mesić assumed his position.

During the summer of 1991, members of the ŠVK began consulting those members of the SIV that still supported the ideals of the SFRJ, or at least acted as if doing so: these were the three representatives of Serbia and one from Montenegro, all of whom were hand-picked by Milošević. From that moment, the generals of the ŠVK were no longer accountable to anyone. The leading man of the team, General Kadijević, then devised an offensive plan against Croatia: during its first phase, the JNA was to 'tolerate' activities of the Croat forces while only carrying out counterattacks of tactical importance. This was to

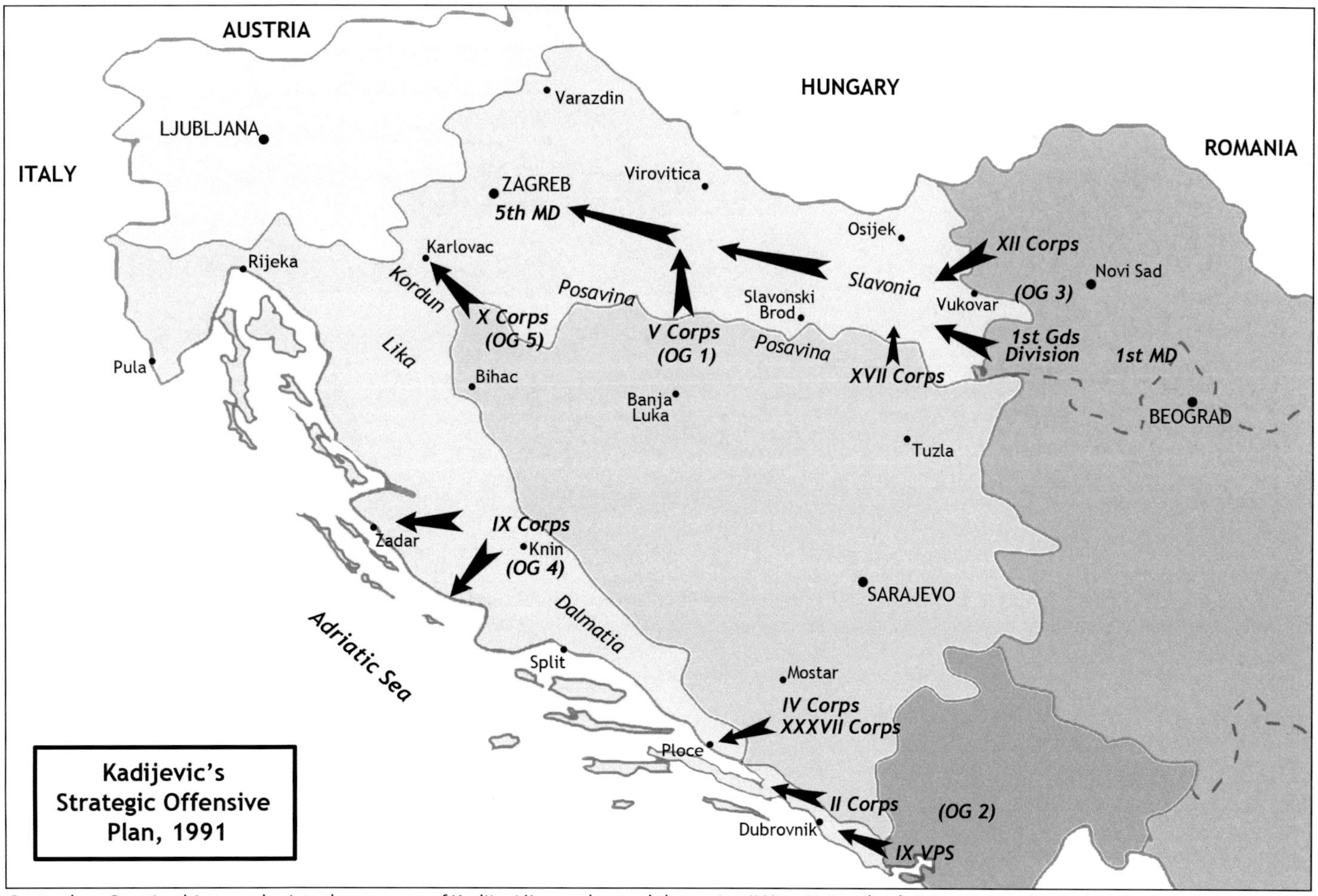

Centred on Croatia, this map depicts the essence of Kadijević's warplan and the major JNA units involved. OGs 1-5 were 'operational groups' which were to be formed from regular JNA units and the TO. IX VPS was Vojno-pomorski sector IX, ground forces originally assigned to the Naval Military District. (Map by Tom Cooper)

Yugoslavia's Electronic Warfare Aircraft

During the first half of 1991, under conditions of stringent security the RV i PVO modified a Mi-8 helicopter and a Yak-40 business jet as platforms for electronic intelligence (ELINT) gathering using equipment acquired from Elletronica (now ELT) from Italy.

A similar plan had emerged already in 1980, when the idea was to rely on technological support from the USA, France, and Sweden. At the time, all available electronic warfare systems in service were ground based: the sole exception being MiG-21Rs with their R-pods, acquired since 1969. Later on, negotiations were opened with the privately owned company Elletronica and in 1985 and 1986 two contracts were signed in great secrecy for acquisition of equipment actually reserved for NATO-members. The first of these related to the installation of ELT-555 pods on Orao fighter-bombers to enable them to penetrate heavily protected combat zones. The second was for the integration of Smart Guard ELINT-systems and Aries-A electronic countermeasures (ECM) equipment into Mi-8s and Yak-40s.

The Yugoslavs were dissatisfied with ELT-555s as these proved to be not completely developed and were technically unreliable. Moreover, manufacturer support was unsatisfactory and correspondingly, this project was abandoned. Nevertheless, the work on the second project was continued. The Yak-40 serial number 71506 was overhauled in the USSR in 1987, and then prepared for modifications. However, Ellectronica was late with its part of the work and began installing and integrating the Smart Guard ELINT systems and the Aries-A ECM systems only in 1989. Indeed, it was only in early 1991 that the resulting Yak-40E was ready.

Meanwhile, between October 1987 and December 1989, four Mi-8s (serials 12409, 12410, 12411, and 12412) were provided to the Moma Stanojlović Works, overhauled and modified through the addition of elements of the Aries-F

At first glance, the modified Yak-40E retained the appearance and livery of a business jet capable of carrying 18 passengers. It is only upon closer inspection that a 'farm' of black antennas for the Smart Guard ELINT system is visible under the fuselage, as are omni-directional antennas of the Aries-A under the wing. Notably, the Soviet-made navigational aids were removed. (Photos by Aleksandar Radić)

ELINT system, which was expanded into an ECM system through the addition of ALQ-6 and ALQ-7 noise jammers, two RMB-7 radar-signal receivers, and the ELT-777 video analyser. Eventually, the Mi-8s in question received the local designation HT-40E. Mi-8s 12410 and 12412 received the full modifications and were to serve as primary platforms, while the 12409 and 12411 lacked some of the equipment (such as the video analyser). The existence of all four helicopters and the modified Yak-40 remained a closely guarded secret and although assigned to the newly-established and specialised unit, the 678th Mixed Aviation Squadron (established on 5 March 1990, homebased at Bihać AB), they retained their standard markings and were almost never shown in public.

Subsequent testing resulted in the RV i PVO developing a plan under which the helicopters would first be used to precisely pinpoint enemy air defences, and then create a 'window' for a penetration by low-flying attack aircraft through jamming enemy radars with the Aries-F.

The Yak-40E formally passed testing at the Aviation Test Centre in February 1991, followed by HT-40Es 12410 and 12412 on 2 July 1991. The other two modified Mi-8s did so only during the autumn of the latter year. Staff of this unit worked hard on developing ELINT- and ECM-tactics, but during the war there was no need for them to provide electronic warfare support. Moreover, the UN arms embargo against the SFRJ terminated the cooperation between Elletronica and the RV i PVO. The unit was withdrawn from Bihać AB and its helicopters split into two flights. Two HT-40Es flew missions along the border with Hungary, while two others operated over western Slavonia from Banja Luka. Their crews spent most of the war eavesdropping on enemy radio and telephone communications: several intercepted recordings were then used for propaganda purposes, revealing entirely unknown capabilities of the Yugoslav intelligence services.

The HT-40E was easily recognisable due to the bulky antennas on its side: the lower portions of these served the ALQ-6 system (covering frequencies of 1-2GHz), and the upper the ALQ-7 (2-4GHz). Above the cabin was the front-transmitting antenna of the Aries-F electronic warfare system (emitting at 2-4GHz), and below the antenna of the RMB-7 ELINT-system. An omni-directional antenna (receiver for frequencies of 0.7-4GHz) was installed low on the left side of the fuselage. Notable in the background to the right is the external landing-light housing, installed in 1997. (Photos by Aleksandar Radic and Zdenko Molnar)

buy time until the TO of the SAO Krajina – or what Kadijević termed the 'Serbian rebels' – was expanded and reorganised with the help of the JNA. Then, the plan was to wait for a Croat attack '...which would make it obvious for everybody who was the attacker and who the defender, who was imposing the war, and who hit back only then.'

At that point in time, the JNA was to establish a complete blockade from the sea and from the air, and then launch an all-out air and ground offensive and defeat the Croat forces, 'fully, if the situation permitted'. This part of the operation was to be conducted in close cooperation with the 'Serbian rebels.' Kadijević planned the counteroffensive to be run in four strategic directions, of which two – once they broke free into the depth of the enemy territory – were to unite. 1st Proletarian Guards Mechanised Division and XII Corps of the JNA were to strike over the Danube into western Slavonia and V Corps was to strike from Banja Luka over the Sava River via Gradiška to Virovitica.

Once these two assault prongs had met, they would turn west and advance on Zagreb and Varaždin, re-connecting with blocked-in elements of X and XXXII Corps, before continuing all the way to the Slovenian border. The third strike was to be run by elements of X Corps JNA, reinforced by units from other parts of the SFRJ, from Bihać via Karlovac to Zagreb. In Dalmatia, IX Corps JNA was supposed to break through to the coastal cities like Zadar, Šibenik and Split, while II Corps, 9th MNS and elements of XXXVII Corps – all advancing from the Mostar area in Bosnia and Herzegovina – were to secure the estuary of the Neretva River and encircle and block the ancient city of Dubrovnik on the Adriatic coast, and keep it besieged as a bargaining chip for further negotiations with Zagreb.

The overall aim was to unblock and extract all the JNA garrisons holding out deep inside Croatia, and to secure the SAO Krajina and then expand the territories under its control. Cut to pieces, Croatia would then be forced into negotiations from the position of the defeated party, and then the JNA was to withdraw entirely.[3]

The reconnaissance version of an Orao aircraft can be seen in the background of this photo, taken at Mostar AB, with a camera pod muunted underneath the fuselage. In the foreground is a trolley of bombs intended for Jastreb aircraft from 240th Squadron. (Dragan Veličković)

Croat War Plan

The opportunity for the realisation of Kadijević's plan offered itself in mid-September, when President Tuđman succumbed to the pressure of hardliners in his cabinet and the party, and ordered the ZNG to besiege all the military bases of the JNA in Croatia. The original idea for such an action had been devised by the Croat Minster of Defence Špegelj during the war in Slovenia and was driven by the desire to obtain arms from the extensive depots of the JNA still in the republic. However, at the time Tuđman refused to follow this proposal fearing open war with the JNA. Instead, he preferred to work on expanding and strengthening the ZNG first. Differences over the two ideas reached a point where Špegelj was fired by Tuđman on 2 July 1991. Nevertheless, planning following his ideas was continued and thus the mass of the ZNG continued its preparations for a general assault on the remaining JNA bases. While still building up, the ZNG began blocking the JNA bases, collecting intelligence about their defences, the ethnic composition of the troops inside, their armament, deployment, and the position of a growing number of mines surrounding them.

By mid-September 1991, the situation was ripe for the assault: clashes with the JNA were a now daily occurrence, Vukovar was besieged, and – because of desertions and a major crisis related to the recruiting for compulsory military service – the majority of besieged bases were short on troops. Indeed, many of the besieged JNA units existed on paper only, and it was only a question of time until their commanders would become sufficiently disheartened to start giving up on their own.

Refined with the help of intelligence provided by officers and other ranks that had defected from the JNA, and also by officers that pretended to be loyal but were in contact with Zagreb, the Croat war plan was fully developed by Generals Špegelj and Tus, and Colonel Agotić during the first half of September 1991. Indeed, Tus was appointed the Chief of Main Staff of the Croat Armed Forces on 14 September, and promptly set his forces in motion.[4]

Trip Wire

The legal basis for the Croat operation was provided on 11 September 1991 by nobody less than President Stipe Mesić. He ordered all Federal forces to suspend their operations in Croatia, and withdraw to their bases, while all armed formations of the SAO Krajina were to be disbanded and disarmed – and in a matter of only 48 hours. Of course, this was an ultimatum nobody in Zagreb expected would be fulfilled by the other side. Unsurprisingly, the Croat government decided to go into action and began distributing related orders on 12 September 1991. Although Tuđman signed his related order only a day later, on the same evening all provision of utility services for JNA bases in Croatia – energy, water, food, sanitary services – was cut off, and the barracks, warehouses and even roads used by the armed forces put under a siege. Moreover, and for the first time ever, the related orders contained the expression 'enemy.'

Of course, by this time the SSNO, the ŠVK, and the entire JNA were no longer listening to the official president of the country for

On 26 April 1991 Captain 1st Class Branislav Dronjak in MiG-21bis serial 17103 swerved from the runway of Bihać AB into a sinkhole. The aircraft was heavily damaged and the pilot was trapped in the cockpit and extracted some ten minutes after the accident. On 17 September 1991, pilot Captain 1st Class Dušan Buban in MiG-21bis 17104 on a combat mission over Varaždin airfield, was hit with a Strela-2M missile. The rear end of aircraft 17013 was used in the repair of 17104, which was reinstated back into service. (117th Brigade)

which they were officially fighting. On the contrary, the senior officers of the armed forces had understood this ultimatum for what it really was: a pretext for an all-out Croat attack on besieged JNA bases. However, acting in this fashion meant that it was the top commanders of the JNA who ended the armed forces' obedience to the formal hierarchy of the SFRJ. This paradox went as far as that, although subsequently continuing to refer its decisions to the 'Presidency of the SFRJ', henceforth, the ŠVK meant by this the truncated composition of Serbia and Montenegro and Kadijević's warplan was actually authorised by the members of the ŠVK only!

Igalo Summit

From that point onward, the formalities did not matter to anybody of importance in what was once the SFRJ. Wherever possible, the JNA bases in Croatia were surrounded by three rings of Croat troops; roadblocks consisting of trucks filled with gravel or gas canisters, construction machinery or – sometimes – anti-tank hedgehogs or concrete pyramids were positioned on all entrances and nearby roads and streets. The first attacks followed once the ultimatum expired (without any official response from Belgrade), and primarily targeted major warehouses. These were poorly protected while the Croat forces needed arms and ammunition. Their tactics were dictated by the fear of air power and small combat teams operated mostly by night, well scattered so to present the least possible target for air strikes. Whenever a warehouse was overrun, it was quickly emptied by civilian trucks, and the loot redistributed to a large number of small depots.

However, major military bases with stronger troop complements proved a much tougher nut to crack. On the contrary, the defenders of many of these managed to repel repeated assaults by their lightly armed and frequently inexperienced opponents. In turn, they were subjected to continuous siege and intensive psychological pressure. The Croats deployed small teams at suitable positions, which then fired at everybody who moved inside, and the troops inside were constantly bombarded with calls to surrender. Special reception centres were established for those who followed such advice – and especially those ready to join the ZNG.

The blockades of barracks resulted in sharp criticism from international mediators in the Yugoslav crisis and under their pressure, and following a meeting in Igalo in Montenegro on 17 September 1991, with Lord Peter Carrington (representative of the EC), President Milošević of Serbia (who also controlled the remnants of the Presidency), and the representatives of the JNA – including Kadijević – Tuđman tried to suspend the activities of his own armed forces. However, hardliners within the HDZ and the Croat armed forces were now in the 'steam locomotive modus', and his order was simply ignored or was declared as a propaganda manoeuvre aimed to appease the foreigners.

A view of Bihać AB during the time of the civil war. About a dozen MiG-21s and two Mi-8s are visible. (Ivan Detiček Collection)

Blockade of the Barracks

One way or another, some bases were quickly overrun, while others held out. The RV i PVO attempted to provide fire-support wherever and whenever possible, or at least to facilitate support through air strikes on nearby ZNG bases. Initially, during the blockade of the bases, the psychological effect of air power was still strong. Siniša Raković, then a commander of an independent company from Podsused (an eastern suburb of Zagreb) recalled that in an attempt to overrun the base and the shooting range at Vrapčanski Potok, on 15 September, there was still a lot of excitement amongst his troops as soon as a jet swooped low over their position and 'at the time we still didn`t know whether that combat aircraft had anything to do with the action around the shooting range, or with the sirens were sounding air raid alert all over Zagreb.' Emboldened by the appearance of the aircraft, the JNA commander refused to surrender and following negotiations his unit was granted safe passage all the way to Serbia.[5]

Such concerns were not only of local nature and in Zagreb, the Croat government expected a large-scale airborne assault on Pleso IAP, and then a combined all-out attack of paratroopers with that of strong units trapped inside their bases around the city, especially 140th Mechanised Brigade in Dugo Selo, and 4th Armoured Brigade in Jastrebarsko. From that point in time, and until the end of the war in 1995, the frontlines of the JNA – and later the Serb forces – were only 20 kilometres south of Pleso. In turn, especially those JNA officers that had been trapped inside their bases for weeks had estimated Croat forces as being strong, numerous, well-armed, and determined to fight. Realistic assessments of the situation inside and outside the besieged bases were rare, and much too often local commanders were not aware of being 'surrounded' by modest forces. Perhaps the worst fate befell the garrison of Varaždin, a town in the northernmost corner of Croatia, where the commands of XXXII Corps and 32nd Mechanised Brigade were stationed. There the officers knew that even an all-out intervention of the JRV i PVO had only minimal chances of success. They surrendered, handing over the biggest pool of armoured vehicles for the ZNG, including a total of 74 T-55 MBTs, 61 M-80 IFVs and M-60 APCs, 36 howitzers of 152mm and 155mm, significant amounts of anti-tank and air defence systems, and their complete stock of tank, artillery, anti-aircraft and small-arms ammunition.

In 1991, one of the prominent leaders of the RV i PVO was Lieutenant Colonel Mahmut Skadrak, a MiG-21-pilot. During the time when pilots were leaving he received an offer from BiH, however he had gaven an oath and did not want to break it. After the war, he went to the USA as a civilian, and then returned to Belgrade. Tragically, he died of cancer in 2012. (Mladen Savić)

RV i PVO against the Blockade

Unlike the JNA, the air force did not lose a single vital facility to the first wave of Croat attacks. Certainly enough, Pleso, Pula, Zemunik, and Divulje, and several major radar positions – with a total of about 2,100 officers and other ranks inside – were all besieged. Reinforced by detachments from 63rd Parachute Brigade, they held out. Other than Pula, a relatively peaceful area that never found itself under direct attack (indeed, where both sides spent most of the war peacefully monitoring each other), Croat forces regularly mortared the bases, and occasionally sent in small teams to penetrate their perimeters. However, all crises were solved with help of air strikes and, for example, all the attacks on Zemunik and Divulje were repelled with help of the air force.

The sense of being besieged soon spread into the Mostar area. Although in Bosnia and Herzegovina, and spared combat operations, the atmosphere in the town and the neighbourhood was very war-like during the autumn of 1991, and the local JRV i PVO garrison

A soldier from the task force of 63rd Parachute Brigade assigned to guard Bihać AB, armed with a Zastava 7.62mm M76 sniper rifle. (Boško Čeliković)

Paratroopers patrol the runway of Bihać AB, which was a lucrative target for potential sabotage operations by the Croatian forces. (Boško Čeliković)

took great care to bolster not only its bases for aircraft in Ortiješ, and for helicopters in Jasenice, but also for the Soko Works which all the time continued assembling Oraos, G-4s, and Gazelles. To bolster the defences, the JNA deployed not only the locally-based 171st Armoured Brigade, but also a battalion of 179th Mountain Brigade from Nikšić in Montenegro and the remnants of 500th Armoured Brigade from Divulje (of which only the 50th Company was still operational). Similarly, the defences of Bihać AB – 70 percent of which was in Croatia and 30 percent in Bosnia and Herzegovina – were reinforced by T-55s of 329th Armoured Brigade from Banja Luka.

Labrador Affair

The situation was dramatically different in the case of the compound that used to house the Command of V Corps JRV i PVO in downtown Zagreb. This was emptied in August, when most officers and other ranks were transferred to Pleso AB. However, security services and some of the administration personnel were still present. On 14 September 1991, the main building was surrounded by well-armed troops, that placed anti-tank obstacles and erected barricades, and then all electricity, water, gas, and telephone links were cut off. Using loudspeakers, the Croats repeatedly demanded a surrender. The 'garrison' inside held out until the next day, when a unit of the Croat Special Police appeared ready to assault the place in an operation aired live on the TV. The police operators quickly broke into the building and arrested all 24 troops still inside. Left without choice, the HQ of V Corps was transferred to the underground Objekt Klek of Bihać AB by several Mi-8s, later the same day.

Despite such losses, the command and control system of the RV i PVO was never interrupted; however, there were serious concerns because the security services had failed to destroy the main archive of the command. Indeed, the Croats found the documentation of the 2nd Detachment CIG, and their intelligence had no problem in reconstructing an entire network of 43 informers and 11 associates of the military security in their political and public life, painstakingly organised over the previous months and years. All were arrested during the following days in the course of what became known as the Labrador Affair. Of the eleven associates, eight were exchanged for Croat prisoners of war in December 1991, while three opted to remain in Croatia.

This is how the war in Yugoslavia converted into the ugly conflict remembered ever since. While the SFRJ thus ceased to exist in its intended form in mid-September 1991, its air force, the RV i PVO was to survive it for another five months – indeed, during the period when it was to see the highest-intensity action, prove its mettle in combat, and also suffer its heaviest losses. That story is to be told in Volume 2 of this project.

Table 7: Aircraft of the JRV i PVO, 27 June 1991		
Unit	**Aircraft Type**	**Serial Number**
		Directly subordinated units
138th Transport Aviation Brigade		
675th Transport Aviation Squadron	Yak-40	71501, 71502, 71504, 71506
	Falcon 50	72101
	LearJet 25	70401, 70402
678th Mixed Aviation Squadron	Do.28D2	70501
	HT-40	12264, 12366
890th Transport Helicopter Squadron	HT-40	12245, 12247, 12265, 12266, 12359, 12362
	HO-45	12892, 12893, 12894
	HO-42	12671
	HI-42	12703
Flight Test Centre	L-17	17101, 17135
	J-22	25101, 25102, 25121, 25152, 25164
	NJ-22	25507
	IJ-22	25714
	N-63	23004, 23686, 23687, 23736
	V-53	53001, 53256
	V-51	51132
676th Fire-Fighting Aviation Squadron	CL.215	72202, 72203, 72205
	HO-45	12896
	HO-42	12622
		I Corps RV i PVO
Liaison Aviation Squadron	HT-40	12207, 12404
	Alouette III	12151, 12152
	HO-45	12880, 12890
	V-51	51111
204th Fighter Aviation Regiment		
126th Fighter Aviation Squadron	L-17	17127, 17134, 17136, 17151, 17152, 17156
	L-17K	17207, 17220, 17225, 17228, 17401, 17406, 17409, 17410
	NL-16	16182, 16185
	NL-12	22906
	V-51	51107, 51134
127th Fighter Aviation Squadron	L-18	18101, 18102, 18103, 18104, 18105, 18106, 18107, 18108, 18109, 18110, 18111, 18112, 18113, 18114
	NL-18	18301, 18302
	V-51	51247
97th Aviation Brigade		
240th Fighter-Bomber Aviation Squadron	J-21	24121, 24126, 24129, 24130, 24145, 24150, 24156, 24203, 24210, 24213, 24254, 24269, 24270
	IJ-21	24405

Table 7: Aircraft of the JRV i PVO, 27 June 1991 *(continued)*

	NJ-21	23501, 23506, 23507
	N-60	23128, 23170, 23186, 23188
	V-51	51142, 51223
252nd Fighter-Bomber Aviation Squadron	J-21	24116, 24122, 24201, 24214, 24220, 24256, 24257, 24259, 24261, 24268
	N-60	23173, 23176, 23177, 23187, 23204, 23257
	N-62	23630, 23645, 23647, 23734
	N-62T	23603, 23606
	V-51	51133
353rd Reconnaissance Aviation Squadron	IJ-22	25716, 25717, 25718, 25719, 25721, 25723, 25724, 25725, 25726
	INJ-22	25601, 25604, 25605
	INJ-22M	25606
790th Transport Helicopter Squadron	HT-40	12237, 12241, 12248, 12302, 12303, 12307, 12309, 12311, 12354, 12361
784th Anti-Submarine Squadron	HP-43	11301, 11305, 11306, 11323
	HP-44	11351, 11352, 11354
	HP-46	11401, 11402
	HT-40	12214, 12261, 12310, 12312
	II Corps RV i PVO	
83rd Fighter Aviation Regiment		
123rd Fighter Aviation Squadron	L-17	17154, 17155, 17157, 17158, 17159, 17160, 17162, 17163, 17164, 17165, 17166
	L-17K	17202, 172017, 17231, 17232, 17408
	NL-16	16158
	NL-14	22957
	NL-12	22907, 22914
	V-51	51140, 51141
130th Fighter Aviation Squadron	L-15	22801, 22803, 22805, 22811, 22813, 22816, 22817, 22818, 22819, 22823 and 22824 re-engined to R13-300 22814 and 22815 still powered by R11F2SK-300
	L-17	17131, 17132
	NL-16	16174
	NL-14	22952
	NL-12	22918
	V-51	51124, 51131
98th Aviation Brigade		
241st Fighter-Bomber Aviation Squadron	J-22	25103, 25104, 25112, 25113, 25118, 25154, 25155, 25156, 25158, 25160, 25161, 25167, 25172, 25173
	NJ-22	25505, 25512 (on loan from 242nd Squadron)
	V-51	51201, 51204 (damaged in heavy landing on 21 Jun 1991 and handed over to the workshop)
247th Fighter-Bomber Aviation Squadron	J-21	24103, 24114, 24119, 24124, 24125, 24128, 24140, 24142, 24144, 24154, 24155, 24206, 24207, 24215, 24252, 24253, 24266, 24274
	NJ-21	23516

Table 7: Aircraft of the JRV i PVO, 27 June 1991 *(continued)*		
	N-60	23113, 23126, 23144
	V-51	51248
354th Reconnaissance Aviation Squadron	IJ-21	24401, 24404, 24409, 24412, 24414, 24415, 24417, 24424, 24427, 24428, 24430, 24451, 24452, 24453, 24454, 24457, 24458
	N-60	23114, 23156, 24167
	V-51	51119, 51203
119th Aviation Brigade	V-51	51118, 51127
677th Transport Aviation Squadron	T-70	71352, 71364, 71371, 71374, 71382
	An-2TD	70371, 70372
712th Anti-Armour Helicopter Squadron	HN-45M	12902, 12904, 12905, 12906, 12907, 12908, 12909, 12910, 12911, 12912, 12914, 12915, 12916, 12917, 12918, 12919
	H-45	12879
714th Anti-Armour Helicopter Squadron	HN-42M	12803, 12805, 12808, 12809, 12810, 12811, 12813, 12815, 12817, 12823, 12827, 12829, 12830, 12833, 12834, 12837
	HO-42	12605
787th Transport Helicopter Squadron	HT-40	12203, 12206, 12209, 12221, 12240, 12246, 12263, 12270, 12272, 12273, 12304, 12353, 12355, 12360, 12367
V Corps RV i PVO		
117th Fighter Aviation Regiment		
124th Fighter Aviation Squadron	L-17	17107, 17109, 17110, 17125, 17129, 17130, 17133, 17170, 17171
	L-17K	17206, 17208, 17212, 17214, 17226, 17229, 17405
	NL-16	16152, 16153, 16177
	NL-14	22953
125th Fighter Aviation Squadron	L-17	17104, 17106, 17126, 17161, 17167, 17169
	L-17K	17201, 17203, 17204, 17205, 17209, 17210, 17211, 17213, 17235, 17407
	NL-16	16179, 16180
	NL-12	22908, 22909
	V-51	51139
352nd Reconnaissance Aviation Squadron	L-14i	26101, 26102, 26104, 26107, 26108, 26109, 26111, 26112
	L-15M	22865, 22866, 22867, 22868
	L-14	22707, 22724, 22735
	NL-14	22951
	V-51	51125
82nd Aviation Brigade		
237th Fighter-Bomber Aviation Squadron	J-21	24111, 24133, 24136, 24139, 24141, 24148, 24158, 24160, 24202, 24205, 24208, 24209, 24212, 24218, 24251, 24258, 24275
	NJ-21	23509, 23511
	N-60	23120, 23133, 23178, 23181, 23182
	V-51	51130
238th Fighter-Bomber Aviation Squadron	J-22	25105, 25106, 25111, 25114, 25115, 25116, 25119, 25122, 25123, 25151 (damaged in a fire on 18 June, but still at Cerklje when the war began), 25153

Table 7: Aircraft of the JRV i PVO, 27 June 1991 (*continued*)		
	NJ-22	25502
	V-51	51128
351st Reconnaissance Aviation Squadron	IJ-22	25709, 25710, 25711, 25712
	NJ-22	25504
	INJ-22	25609
	IJ-21	24406, 24407, 24410, 24421, 24423, 24425, 24429, 24456
	N-60	23158, 23212
111th Aviation Brigade		
679th Transport Aviation Squadron	T-70	71351, 71359, 71366, 71369, 71377, 71379, 71385
	An-2TD	70373
	V-51	51117, 51143
711th Anti-Armour Helicopter Squadron	HN-42M	12806, 12807, 12812, 12818, 12819, 12820, 12821, 12822, 12824, 12825, 12826, 12828, 12831, 12832, 12835, 12836
	HO-42	12612
713th Anti-Armour Helicopter Squadron	HN-45M	12921, 12922, 12923, 12924
	HO-45	12877
780th Transport Helicopter Squadron	HT-40	12204, 12205, 12213, 12216, 12219, 12222, 12224, 12239, 12244, 12262, 12268, 12271, 12403, 12405, 12406, 12407, 12408 (shot down 27 Jun 1991)
		Air Force Academy
105th Fighter-Bomber Aviation Regiment (Training)		
249th Fighter-Bomber Aviation Squadron (Training)	N-62	23648, 23649, 23691, 23692, 23725, 23726, 23727, 23728, 23732, 23733, 23735, 23738, 23739, 23740
	V-53	53172, 53214, 53246, 53247, 53248, 53250, 53254, 53255, 53259, 53260
	V-51	51144
251st Fighter-Bomber Aviation Squadron (Training)	N-60	23119, 23121, 23136, 23137, 23147, 23148, 23149, 23150, 23151, 23152, 23157, 23163, 23164, 23165, 23166, 23168, 23171, 23180, 23185, 23190, 23191, 23197, 23199
	N-60	23112, 23128, 23153, 23154, 23155, 23179, 23189, 23207 (all out of resources)
	V-53	53156, 53244, 53245, 53249, 53251, 53252, 53253, 53257, 53258, 53261
	V-51	51222
333rd Fighter-Bomber Aviation Squadron (Training)	N-60	23180, 23194, 23196, 23205, 23206, 23208, 23211, 23251, 23252, 23254, 23255, 23256, 23258, 23259, 23260, 23261, 23263, 23264, 23265, 23268
	N-62	23693, 23694, 23695, 23696, 23697, 23698, 23699 (all with the aerobatic team Letece zvezde)
	An-2TD	70375
	HO-45	12891
172nd Fighter-Bomber Aviation Regiment (Training)		
239th Fighter-Bomber Squadron (Training)	N-62	23650, 23675, 23676, 23677, 23679, 23680, 23681, 23683, 23685, 23689, 23690, 23700, 23729, 23730, 23731, 23737, 23741, 23742 (23657 and 23677 undergoing modifications at Soko)
242nd Fighter-Bomber Squadron (Training)	J-22	25163, 25166, 25168, 25169, 25170, 25171, 25174, 25175, 25201, 25202

Table 7: Aircraft of the JRV i PVO, 27 June 1991 *(continued)*		
	NJ-22	25506, 25508, 25509, 25511, 25512 (loaned to 241st Squadron), 25525, 25526, 25527, 25528, 25529, 25530 (undergoing repairs at Golubovci following in-flight fire on 21 Jun 1991), 25531
	NJ-21	23510, 23512, 23518
	V-51	51115, 51181
	HO-45	12878
185th Fighter-Bomber Aviation Regiment (Training)		
129th Fighter Aviation Squadron (Training)	NL-16	16151, 16154, 16171, 16173, 16175, 16176, 17178
	L-14	22701, 22703, 22705, 22712, 22719, 22720, 22725, 22729, 22731, 22732, 22733, 22736
	V-51	51103, 51184
229th Fighter-Bomber Squadron (Training)	N-62	23624, 23625, 23626, 23627, 23628, 23629, 23631, 23632, 23635, 23636, 23637, 23638, 23640, 23641, 23642, 23643, 23644
	V-51	51183
	NSn-45	12895
107th Mixed Aviation Regiment (Training)		Reorganised as the Aviation Regiment (Training) on 28 Jun 1991
722nd Anti-Armour Helicopter Squadron (Training)	HN-45M	12920, 12925, 12927, 12928, 12929, 12930, 12931, 12932, 12933, 12934, 12935, 12936, 12937, 12938, 12939, 12940, 12941; unit disbanded on 28 Jun 1991, all equipment transferred to 782nd Squadron
	HT-40	12208, 12211, 12215, 12218, 12220, 12223, 12267, 12305, 12313 and 12369
782nd Helicopter Squadron (Training)	H-42	12604; 12609, 12611, 12614, 12615, 12616, 12619, 12631, 12633, 12634, 12635, 12662, 12666 and 12801
	HSn-42	12754, 12755
Units subordinated to MD commands		
891st Reconnaissance and Liaison Aviation Squadron (3rd MD), 1st Flight	HO-42	12607
	HO-45	12872
	Hi-42	12704, 12713, 12720
891st Reconnaissance and Liaison Aviation Squadron (3rd MD), 2nd Flight	HO-42	12618
	HO-45	12871
	HI-42	12712, 12719
891st Reconnaissance and Liaison Aviation Squadron (3rd MD), 3rd Flight	HO-42	12617, 12663
	HO-45	12875
	HI-42	12710, 12717
894th Reconnaissance and Liaison Aviation Squadron (5th MD), 1st Flight	HO-42	12606, 12665, 12667
	HO-45	12873, 12882
	HI-42	12707, 12709
894th Reconnaissance and Liaison Aviation Squadron (5th MD), 2nd Flight	HO-42	12660, 12664
	HI-42	12718
895th Reconnaissance and Liaison Aviation Squadron (Naval MD)	HI-42	12702, 12715

Table 7: Aircraft of the JRV i PVO, 27 June 1991 *(continued)*

	HSn-42	12756
	HO-45	12874
896th Reconnaissance and Liaison Aviation Squadron (1st MD), 1st Flight	HO-42	12613
	HI-42	12705, 12711, 12721
	HO-45	12881
896th Reconnaissance and Liaison Aviation Squadron (1st MD), 2nd Flight	HO-42	12668, 12672
	HI-42	12708, 12716
	H-45	12876
Montenegro TO Squadron	J-20	30131, 30136, 30139, 30147, 30151, 30155, 30157
	V-51	51116
ATC Flight	Yak-40	71503, 71505
Zmaj Works	L-17	17218 (handed to 126th Squadron on 4 Jul), 17215 (30%), 17221 (8%), 17222 (returned to 126th Squadron due to the war, 4 Jul 1991), 17223 (10%), 17224 (45%), 17227 (85%, handed over to 126th Squadron on 4 Jul), 17233 (10%), 17404 (55%)[6]
	L-14	22704 (overhaul interrupted, returned to 129th Squadron on 12 Jun 1991)
	L-14i	26103 (75%), 26105 (70%)
	NL-16	16155 (overhaul interrupted; returned to 126th Squadron on 7 Jul 1991)
	NL-14	22955 (8%)
	N-62	23621 (65%), 23622 (50%), 23623 (overhaul pending)
	N-62T	23004 (complete), 23005 (65%), 23601 (repairs), 23602 (5%), 23604 (70%), 23605 (15%)
	J-21	24272 (complete, returned to 252nd Squadron on 4 Jul 1991), 24105 (60%), 24158 (repairs)
	NJ-21	23513 (modification into naval reconnaissance aircraft abandoned, returned to unit due to war)
	N-60	23111 (7%), 23118 (overhaul pending sale to Indonesia), 23128 (50%), 23153 (35%), 23154 (60%), 23155 (13%), 23179 (work abandoned, returned to unit on 4 Jul 1991), 23183 (35%), 23189 (work pending), 23207 (5%), 23210 and 23266 (work complete and handed to 252nd Squadron on 4 Jul 1991)
	MiG-21IQ	21174 (50%), 21177 (20%), 21186 (70%), 21190 (45%), 21206 (65%), 21168, 21198, 21204 completed and handed over to 126th Squadron in early Jul 1991
	MiG-23ML	23252 (6%), 23260 (55%), 23267 (60%), 23269 (complete), 23272 (2%), 23278 (35%), 23279 (45%), 23288 (40%), 23290 (30%), 23292 (70%)
Moma Stanojlović Works	J-22	25117 (10% of repairs)
	IJ-22	25701 (45%), 25702 (45%), 25703 (55%), 25704 (20%), 25706 (25%), 25707 (work pending), 25708 (100%), 25715 (work pending)
	INJ-22	25602 (work pending)
	J-21	24204 (10%), 24260 (10%)
	IJ-21	24408 (7%), 24418 and 24422 (work pending)
	NJ-21	23502 (7%), 23505 (work pending)
	N-60	23123 (overhaul pending sale to the US civilian market)
	T-70	71362 (35%), 71386 (7%)
	Yak-40	71506 (95% modification for ELINT purposes)

Table 7: Aircraft of the JRV i PVO, 27 June 1991 *(continued)*		
	An-2TD	70374 (95%)
	CL.215	72204 (95%, returned to 676th Squadron on 7 Jul 1991)
	V-51	51109 (10%), 51145 (7%), 51146 (95%), 51182 (100%), 51202 (7%), 51221 (0%), 51225 (10%), 51246 received from TOS), 51134 (received from 126th Squadron)
	V-53 (from VSJ)	53002 (95%), 53102 (5%), 53124 (95%), 53158 (5%), 53163 (0%), 53200 (5%), 53204 (10%), 53205 (100%), 53213 (7%), 53228 (5%), 53232 (7%), 53237 (5%), 53240 (90%)
	V-53 (from RV i PVO)	53241 (5%), 53242 (60%)
	HT-40	12212 (7%), 12262 (15%), 12269 (10%), 12308 (75%), 12352 (15%), 12364 (10%), 12365 (work pending), 12368 (10%), 12370 (95%), 12402 (7%)
	HT-40E	undergoing upgrade to ELINT-version, 12410 and 12412 (both handed to 678th Squadron on 2 Jul 1991), 12409 and 12411 (80%)
	H-42	12620 (95%), 12651 (10%), 12652 (10%), 12653 (10%), 12654 (10%), 12655 (7%), 12657 (3%), 12658 (10%), 12659 (work pending) , 12661 (10%), 12669 (work pending)
	HSn-42	12752 (90%), 12753 (5%)
	HN-42M	12804 (5%)
	N-61/Zlin 526[7]	41111 (35%), 41116 (100%), 41118 (35%), YU-CDG/41276 (100%)
	HT-41/Mi-2[8]	12502, 12503, 12505, 12508
Soko Works	J-22	Undergoing modifications, 2510725108, 25110, 25120, 25124
	NJ-22	Undergoing modifications, 22501, 22503
171st Air Base	NJ-21	23514 (undergoing repairs)
	V-51	51185 (pending overhaul at Moma Stanojlović Works)
770th Plant, Kacha (USSR/Ukraine)[9]	Ka-25PL	11302, 11324

BIBLIOGRAPHY

Aralica, Tomislav, Čopec Robert, Jeras Marko, Kinjerovac Zdenko i Haraminčić Tomislav, *Sto godina ratnog zrakoplovstva u Hrvatskoj* (Zagreb: Hrvatska Povijest, 2012)

Boflek, Boris, *Teritorialna obramba kot oblika vojaške organizacije*, (Ljubljana: PhD thesis, Univerza v Ljubljani, 2010)

Bošković, Rajica, *Nebo na dlanu* (Beograd: self-published, 2017)

Ćurik, Damir, *Let helikoptera 7303 za Knin* (Zagreb: Branitelji Hrvatske, 2010)

Cvetko, Simon, *Delovanje območnih štabov teritorialne obrambe od ustanovitve do konca oboroženih spopadov – primer 83. območni štab* (Ljubljana: Univerza v Ljubljani, Fakulteta za družbene vede, 2016)

Dimitrijević, Bojan, *Kurjaci sa Ušća* (Beograd: ISI, 2004)

Dimitrijević, Bojan, *Tito's Underground Air Base: Bihać Underground Yugoslav Air Force Base, 1964-1992* (Warwick: Helion & Co., 2018)

Džamić, Dragan, *30 godina Specijalne antiterorističke jedinice* (Beograd: Ministarstvo Unutrašnjih Poslova, 2008)

Grčar, Jure, *Napad Jugoslovanske ljudske armade na letališče Brnik* (Ljubljana: PhD thesis, Univerza v Ljubljani, Fakulteta za družbene vede, 2010)

Gregurić, Franjo, *Vlada demokratskog jedinstva* (Zagreb: Školska Knjiga i Hanza Media, 2017)

Horvat, Mladen, *Gradivo za študijo primera oboroženega spopada na terenu: Potek vojne za Slovenijo 1991 na smeri Ormož-Gornja Radgona* (Ljubljana: Generlštab Slovenske Vojske, 2018)

Horvat, Mladen, *Teritorialna obramba Vzhodnoštajerske pokrajine (7. PŠTO) v vojni za Slovenijo 1991* (Maribor: PhD thesis, Univerza v Mariboru, 2015)

Javorović, Božidar, *Narodna zaštita grada Zagreba u Domovinskom ratu* (Zagreb: Defimi, 1999)

Jelić Ivo, *Čovjek i rat* (Split: Hrvatski Časnički Zbor Grada Splita, 2005)

Jereb, Vojislav i Frka, Danijel, *Hrvatski zrakoplovi* (Zagreb: Carski Husar, 1994)

Jerič, Jožef, *Prvih oseminštiredeset ur, ko je šlo zares...* (Brežice: *Spoominski zbornik Posavje v letih 1989-1991*)

Kadijević, Veljko, *Moje viđenje raspada* (Beograd: Politika, 1993)

Kadijević, Veljko, *Protiv udar* (Beograd: IP Filip Višnjić, 2010)

Karan, Ljuban, *Bio sam oficir KOS-a* (Beograd: Blic, 2006)

Kolšek, Konrad, *Prvi pucanj u SFRJ – Sećanja na početak oružanih sukoba u Sloveniji i Hrvatskoj* (Beograd: Dan Graf, 2005)

Kronika '91: Put do suverenosti (Ljubljana: Adria Airways, 1992)

Krstić, Vladica, *Vojnici sa dve zakletve* (Beograd: NIC Vojska, 2005)

Marijan, Davor, *Slom Titove armije* (Zagreb: Golden Marketing-Tehnička Knjiga i Hrvatski Institut za Povijest, 2008)

Naglić, Janja, *Vojna na Koroškem leta 1991* (Ljubljana: PhD thesis, Fakultet za družbene vede, 2008)

Najman, Dujić, Posilović, *Bloklade i osvajanje vojarni i vojnih objekata JNA u Hrvatskoj* (Zagreb: Udruga dragovoljaca Narodne zašstite Domovinskog rata, 2004)

Najman, Dujić, Posilović, *Bloklade i osvajanje vojarni i vojnih objekata JNA u Hrvatskoj – grad Zagreb* (Zagreb: Udruga dragovoljaca Narodne zašstite Domovinskog rata, 2005)

Nanut, Karlo, *Uporaba in delovanje oklepno-mehaniziranih enot JLA* (Ljubljana: Vojaška zgodovina št 1/05)

Ožbalt, Fajmunt: *Vojna na Koroškem – operativno vodenje bojnih delovanj* (Ljubljana: Vojaška zgodovina št. 1/06)

Pilić, Stipo, *Jedan pogled na bitku za Vukovar* 1991 (www.croatiarediviva.com/2016/11/22/jedan-pogled-bitku-vukovar-1991/)

Potočnjak, Draga, *Skrito povelje* (Ljubljana: Založba Sanje, 2013)

Predojević, Vaso, *U procjepu* (Beograd: Dan Graf, 1997)

Prva Gardijska brigada Hrvatske vojske Tigrovi (Zagrb: Znanje, 2015)

Radić, Aleksandar and Hrelja, Mario, *Soko J-20 Kraguj* (Beograd: Naša krila, 2019)

Rajtar, Vladimir, *Nebeski ratnici* (Zagreb: self-published, 1995)

Remškar, Sanja, *Občina Vrhnika v času Vojne za Slovenijo (1991)* (Ljubljana: PhD thesis, Univerza v Ljubljani, Filozofska Fakulteta, Fakulteta za družbene vedem, 2007)

Spasojević, Dragoslav, *Poslednji zaokret, Pilotske priče* (Beograd: self-published, 2018)

Špegelj, Martin, *Sjećanja vojnika* (Zagreb: Znanje, 2001)

Stodeseta, (Karlovac: Udruga pripadnika 110. brigade ZNG-HV, 2007)

Švajcner, Janez, *Odbranili domovino* (Ljubljana: Viharnik, 1993)

Vasiljević, Aleksandar, *Štit, akcija vojne bezbednosti* (Beograd: IGAM, 2012)

Višnjić, F., *Protiv Udar* (Beograd: IP Filip Višnjić, 2010)

Vojno tužilaštvo pri SSNO, br. 341/91 od 30.1.1992. OPTUŽNICA protiv Trifunović Vlade general-majora, Raduški Sretena, pukovnika, Popov Berislava, pukovnika, davidović Vladimira, potpukovnika, Lukić Miloša, potpukovnika, Malinić Zorana, kapetana, Jovanov Gorana, potporučnika i Magazin Radenka, vodnika I klase

Vuletić, Bernard, *PZO Dalmacije 1991-1992* (Split: self-published, 1996)

Documentation

Documents from the Military Archive, Belgrade, Aeronautical Museum in Surcin, and Command of the JRV i PVO.

NOTES

Chapter 1

1. The Serbian Army had operated aircraft since 1912 when six pilots were trained in France, and Blériot XI and Henry Farman HF.20 aircraft were acquired. A unit of four aircraft took part in the First Balkan War of 1912-1913, flying reconnaissance (first sortie was flown by a two-seater Blériot XI-2 on 29 March 1913). Due to bad weather, this unit did not operate during the Second Balkan War of 1913. Nevertheless, Serbian pilots did fly the first combat operations of the First World War on 13 August 1914. In turn, all of their aircraft were destroyed during the Austro-Hungarian offensive on Serbia in autumn 1915. A new, Franco-Serb unit was established in summer 1916, and expanded to two squadrons during the first half of 1918.
2. Informburo was the Yugoslav name for the 'Communist Information Bureau' (or 'Cominform') – a Moscow-controlled central organization of the International Communist Movement – in 1947-1956.
3. Yugoslav types like Galeb-2, Galeb-4, and similar are generally known under significantly different designations, some of which were based on Belgrade's attempts to market them abroad, and some on misunderstanding. For example, the Galeb-2 is frequently referred to as 'G-2', and the Galeb-4 as 'G-4 Super Galeb': the RV i PVO never used such designations in its documentation. Indeed, to add to the confusion: G-4 was the project and factory designation, while, for example, the air force did use the J-21 designation for the Jastreb. Moreover, the Soko factory used designations like Galeb-1 (prototype), Galeb-2 (series production), Libyan Galeb-2AL, Modernised Galeb-3 and similar. For reasons of simplicity, these three types will be named 'G-2', 'G-4', and 'J-21' in this book.
4. The JNA issued relatively unimaginative names for its plans and operations: Deneb was named after a star in the Cygnus constellation, while most of the other names were based on the season of the year, specific geographic terms, or symbols important to the SFRJ.
5. Interview provided to author on condition of anonymity.

Chapter 2

1. Oplenac is a hill near the town of Topola in central Serbia. At the top of that hill (337m above sea level) is a memorial church and mausoleum of the Karađorđević dynasty.
2. In summer 1991, Agotić became the Chief of Staff of the Croatian Armed Forces.
3. Until 1990, the High Command JRV i PVO exercised direct control over one squadron operating MiG-21R reconnaissance fighters. However, this unit (based at Bihać AB), was then re-assigned to its neighbouring fighter aviation regiment.
4. For details on Objekt Klek and Bihac AB in general, see the sister volume in the Europe@War series *Tito's Underground Air Base*.
5. Because of the war and subsequent developments, the latter – G-4-related – project was realised only in 1999.
6. Reports of an armed Gazelle variant named 'Partisan' were based on a massive misunderstanding by foreign journalists.
7. Hočevar was the best pilot in the 7th Class VVA, which graduated in 1953. He was a flight instructor in the RV i PVO and an officer in various positions in educational and political work, and from 1987 he had led the TD in his home Slovenia. After his dismissal by the Slovenian authorities, Hočevar was called to Belgrade and was appointed to the position of Deputy Chief of General Staff for the RV i PVO. He remained in active service during the civil war until retiring on 25 February 1992.
8. At the beginning of October 1990 there was no longer the need for MSNZ and it was integrated into the TO.
9. Later, during the summer and fall of 1991, a myth emerged that the Croats used large quantities of Stinger missiles. Official documents of the RV and PSC stated that aircraft had been shot down or hit with Stinger missiles because the perception was that the Croats had received strong support from the West and that their combat efficiency was based on modern missiles. Also, for public opinion, this was an acceptable explanation.
10. Damir Ćurik, *Let helikoptera 7303 za Knin* (Zagreb: Branitelji Hrvatske, 2010)
11. In a highly decentralized structure of internal affairs in SFRY, prior to the civil war, the Federal Secretariat for Internal Affairs and the six federal units' Secretariats for Internal Affairs had air units. The SSUP had two AB.212s and one SA 341H Gazelle; Slovenia had one AB.412, one AB.212 and one A.109 and two AB.206B Jet Ranger IIIs; Croatia had one AB.212, one AB.206B Jet Ranger II and two Bell 206B Jet Ranger IIIs (and one was added in March 1991); Bosnia-Herzegovina had two Bell 222B, one Bell 206B Jet Ranger III and one Bell 206L Long Ranger II; Serbia had two AB.212, two SA 365N, one Bell 206L Long Ranger II, 5 Bell 206B Jet Ranger IIIs (and another was added in May 1991) and one SA 341H Gazelle; Montenegro had one AB.212, one AB.206A Jet Ranger I (and one SA 341H Gazelle from June 1991); and Macedonia had one AB.212 and one AB.206B Jet Ranger II.
12. Veljko Kadijević, *Moje viđenje raspada* (Beograd: Politika, 1993) and F Višnjić, *Protiv Udar* (Beograd: IP Filip Višnjić, 2010).

Chapter 3

1. During the war months, the RV i PVO was led by Jurjević, of Croat origin, but who was extraordinarily awarded the second star on 28 November 1991, and Mirčetić who was also extraordinarily awarded the second star on 22 December 1991.
2. In the SFRJ, 'Muslims' were recognised as a separate ethnic group. In the 1990s, the term 'Bosniaks' was introduced instead, which is nowadays in widespread use and considered politically correct. Notably, Skradak was a Muslim who decided to declare himself a Serb.
3. Janez Švajcner: *Odbranili domovino* (Ljubljana: Viharnik, 1993), pp. 18
4. Švajcner, pp. 13-17
5. Aleksandar Radić and Mario Hrelja, *Soko J-20 Kraguj* (Beograd: Naša krila, 2019), pp. 146-152
6. Documentary film *TO-001 Velenje*, TV Studio of Ministry of Defence of Slovenia, www.youtube.com/watch?v=yF_whz6twfI
7. Jožef Jerič, *Prvih oseminštiredeset ur, ko je šlo zares...* (Brežice: *Spoominski zbornik Posavje v letih 1989-1991*)
8. Jerič
9. *TO-001 Velenje*
10. Vladica Krstić, *Vojnici sa dve zakletve* (Beograd: NIC Vojska, 2005)
11. Jerič
12. Draga Potočnjak, *Skrito povelje* (Ljubljana: Založba Sanje, 2013)
13. Revija Obramba
14. Švajcner, pp. 42-44
15. Krstić
16. *Večer* and *TO-001 Velenje*
17. *Kronika '91: Put do suverenosti* (Ljubljana: Adria Airways, 1992)
18. Ožbalt Fajmut: *Vojna na Koroškem – operativno vodenje bojnih delovanj* (Ljubljana: Vojaška zgodovina št. 1/06)
19. Vladimir Rajtar, *Nebeski ratnici* (Zagreb: self-published, 1995)

20. Rajica Bošković, *Nebo na dlanu* (Beograd: self-published, 2017)
21. Konrad Kolšek, *Prvi pucanj u SFRJ – Sećanja na početak oružanih sukoba u Sloveniji i Hrvatskoj* (Beograd: Dan Graf, 2005)
22. Kadijević
23. Dragoslav Spasojević, *Poslednji zaokret, Pilotske priče* (Beograd: self-published, 2018)
24. Rajtar

Chapter 4

1. Later during the war, misinformation appeared in the Serbian media that '20 German instructors had been killed' in Novi Čakovci and that 'a rocket base had been destroyed'. In the fall of 1991 the security service`s propaganda team OPERA, from the Command of the RV i PVO, ran into a media story about Germans killed in the attack by 252nd FBAS. In 1994, Lieutenant-Colonel Radenko Radojčić told the Croatian Secret Service (SZUP) during an investigation, that misinformation had been prepared based on 'some interesting media information' and then an 'intriguing article' would be prepared. In the case of Novi Čakovci, the name of a German citizen who was killed as a volunteer in the Croat forces was used and the topic was expanded and published through a journalist who was an associate of the RV i PVO's security service. Radojčić said that "Such information intrigued the journalists of the ARD (German media house), who jumped on the topic, and then they could have marketed it to our needs because they could actually check that this German existed and died". The statement of Radojčič was published in the Croatian magazine *National Security and the Future* 3-4.2009
2. Najman, Dujić i Posilović, *Bloklade i osvajanje vojarni i vojnih objekata JNA u Hrvatskoj* (Zagreb: Udruga dragovoljaca Narodne zaštite Domovinskog rata, 2004)
3. Formally, by order of the Command of RV i PVO of 6 October 1991, 111th ABDE and 713th ATHS were disbanded, and 111th HR was formed, with units from Zalužani – 780th THS and 711th ATHS. The deadline for the re-forming was 12 October, and the Regiment Formation Ceremony was held on 21 October.
4. Stipo Pilić, *Jedan pogled na bitku za Vukovar* 1991 (www.croatiarediviva.com/2016/11/22/jedan-pogled-bitku-vukovar-1991/)
5. In August 1991 a Vinten 3100/2700 video-camera was installed on J-21 Jastreb aircraft number 24159 for filming the terrain in the area of Slavonia and Baranja. The system consisted of a model 3100 video-camera, with focus length 25mm, 577 x 388 pixels, and a view field of 20° x 16°, an aircraft video-recorder model 2700, which used 30 minute VHS-C cassettes, and a ground video-recorder and a JVC monitor for analyses of recordings.

Chapter 5

1. Dimitrijević, *Kurjaci sa Ušća* (Beograd: ISI, 2004) pp. 27, states that on one occasion the commander of 97th BDE (the name of Colonel Živomir Ninković was deliberately avoided) visited 252nd FBAS in Banja Luka, after the fighting stopped in Slovenia, and ordered the pilots to board the aircraft and sit ready for flight. They stayed in the aircraft for an hour and a half. The nonsensical order was the reason for the conflict and the brigade commander never came back to 252nd FBAS.
2. The document *War Path of the 252nd FBAS* quotes air strikes on 3, 7, and 8 September. The SSNO was more precise and cited that on 7 September on 2310hrs, two aircraft of the RV i PVO encountered ground fire while underway over Čepin airfield, and then returned to fire back. On 8 September at 1040hrs, fire was once again opened on two aircraft in the area of the airfield and they fired back. On 8 September jets underway on reconnaissance spotted 10 An-2s and 2 Dromaders on the airfield in Varaždin, 5 An-2s in Čakovec and 10 An-2s in Čepin. At 1140hrs, a flight of four An-2 aircraft was spotted flying from Beli Manastir-Valpovo, which is where they landed on a provisional airfield. During the night, from 1840hrs to 2010hrs, flights of 14 aircraft were recorded in the regions of Belišće, Valpovo, Podravska Slatina, Beli Manastir, and Apatin, and two An-2 aircraft flew from Yugoslavia to Hungary near Donji Miholjac.

   According to RV i PVO data, on 10 September, from 1930hrs to 2400hrs, 19 small groups of aircraft flew from the depth of Hungary in the direction of Pécs (Slavic Pécs) – Beremend to the very border at 2.5 km. The SSNO states that Hungary was directly involved in the supply of weapons and allowed Croatian forces to use its airports. Furthermore, it was stated that in late August the Hungarian air defence deployed SAM system near the border south of a place called Villány and that the zone of destruction of that system was up to 40km from the border. According to the position of the SSNO, the SAM system was installed as protection for the activities of aircraft from Croatia.
3. Dimitrijević, *Kurjaci sa Ušća*, pp. 39

Chapter 6

1. In June 2018 fishermen found the left the wing and parts of a Galeb-2 on the island of Ugljan.
2. *Narodna armija*, 23 October 1991, *Let na granici svesti*
3. Kadijevićić
4. Most literature quotes 21 September 1991 as the day General Tus was appointed to that position. However, Zagreb announced this decision one day after the adoption of the Croat Law on Defence, on 13 September.
5. Najman, Dujić i Posilović: *Bloklade i osvajanje vojarni i vojnih objekata JNA u Hrvatskoj – grad Zagreb* (Zagreb: Udruga dragovoljaca Narodne zaštite Domovinskog rata, 2005)
6. Percentage figures in brackets denotes the degree to which the overhaul was completed.
7. Type was provided by the RV i PVO to civilian aero-clubs.
8. Withdrawn from service and sold to private owners.
9. Two Ka-25PLs were sent for overhaul in the USSR, but never returned. RV i PVO's standard procedure for aircraft sent for overhauls abroad was to erase them from the registry.

ABOUT THE AUTHOR

Aleksandar Radić is a Serbian military analyst and author. His primary focus is on the security topics of the West Balkans, the history of the armed forces and military technology in that region in the 20th Century, and conflicts that followed the break-up of Yugoslavia, in the 1991-2001 period.

He has authored a dozen books and hundreds of magazine articles published in the specialized press. Recently, Radic frequently appears as military commentator for major TV stations in Serbia, Montenegro, Bosnia and Herzegovina, and the Republic of Northern Macedonia. This is his first book for Helion's @War series.